D0544907

a little taste of…

morocco

a little taste of...

morocco

Recipes and text by Tess Mallos

Photography by
Ashley Mackevicius (recipes)
Martin Brigdale (location)

MURDOCH BOOKS

contents

SPECIAL FEATURES

a little taste...

With its fertile land and rich, colourful history, one would expect Morocco to have an exciting and varied cuisine — and it does not disappoint. Phoenicians and Carthaginians, Romans and Byzantines all had their time in what is now Morocco, but it was the forces of Islam erupting from Arabia in the late seventh century that had the most enduring influence on the culture, including its cuisine.

Of these influences, the introduction of new spices gave Moroccan cuisine its exotic and fragrant flavours and aromas, for which it is renowned. Spices included cinnamon, ginger, saffron, pepper, coriander and cumin, all used to give flavour to the traditional Moroccan tagine, or stew. As other spices from the New World made their appearance — paprika, allspice and chilli — these, too, found their place to add colour and bite.

There are four Moroccan dishes that define the cuisine. Couscous — light, fluffy semolina grains crowned with colourful vegetables and tender, flavoursome lamb or chicken, with a spicy broth to moisten it; *djej emshmel* — a tagine of chicken simmered with preserved lemon and olives to sublime tenderness; *bisteeya* — a pie of slow-cooked chicken or pigeon with lemony, velvety eggs, enclosed in the lightest, flakiest pastry and usually served at banquets; and *mechoui* — lamb rubbed with spices and garlic and slowly spit-roasted until it is so tender it can be 'carved' with the fingers. The characteristic common to all is that they are slow-cooked. Only with slow-cooking can food develop its flavours, and meat or poultry become tender enough to literally fall off the bones.

Tagines and couscous are redolent with herbs and vegetables, with chickpeas sometimes added for extra protein. Fruits such as quinces, apricots, raisins and prunes give a pleasant sweet–sour flavour to some dishes, a concept introduced by the Arabs via Persia, although the indigenous Berbers had always used dates with meat and fish. Vegetable dishes and salads are served at the beginning of a meal and are usually left on

the table to be picked at with the main course. Even these have special touches that can only be Moroccan — a sprinkling of orange flower water and cinnamon on an orange salad, cumin with beetroot, paprika and cumin with carrots…

Sweet pastries are a feature of special occasions — almond-filled pastries such as *kaab el ghzal*, or 'gazelle's horns'; *m'hanncha*, an almond filo 'snake'; and almond briouats dipped in boiling honey — all fragrant with cinnamon and rosewater or orange flower water, with glasses of hot mint tea to follow.

These are some of the tastes and flavours of Moroccan cuisine — on the one hand, a little exotic and mysterious, but on the other, certainly achievable in your own kitchen.

a little taste of...

Where there is meat grilling over charcoal fires, aromas assail the senses. Moroccan bread, filled with tender cubes of lamb fragrant with spices, is very tempting indeed. The *sfenj* (doughnut) makers expertly fry circles of yeast dough to crisp, golden brown perfection. The hot doughnuts are strung on a loop of palm frond for easy carrying, to be eaten dipped in sugar or honey. In city squares and *souks*, open-air markets, there are many such stalls. Long tables laden with colourful salads, flavoursome tagines and steaming couscous, all served by white-garbed men to customers seated on benches. *Harira*, chickpea and lamb soup, is ladled out of simmering cauldrons into pottery bowls to be sipped from lemon-wood spoons. From trolleys and stalls, hot chickpeas are served in paper cones, with a paper square of salt and cumin for sprinkling. In places such as the famous Djemma el Fna, the central square of Marrakesh, the enjoyment of street food is heightened by the spectacle of musicians, dancers, acrobats and snake charmers, all performing around the fringes.

...street food

kefta briouats

1 tablespoon olive oil
1 small onion, finely chopped
350 g (12 oz) lean minced (ground) lamb
2 garlic cloves, crushed
1 tablespoon ground cumin
1 teaspoon ground ginger
1 teaspoon paprika
1 teaspoon ground cinnamon
pinch of saffron threads, soaked in
  a little warm water
1 teaspoon harissa (page 250), or to taste

2 tablespoons chopped coriander
  (cilantro) leaves
2 tablespoons chopped flat-leaf
  (Italian) parsley
1 egg
6–8 sheets filo pastry
90 g (3¼ oz) butter, melted
1 tablespoon sesame seeds

Makes 12

Heat the oil in a large frying pan, add the onion and cook over low heat for 5 minutes, or until the onion is soft. Increase the heat, add the lamb and garlic and cook for 5 minutes, breaking up any lumps with the back of a wooden spoon. Add the spices, harissa and the chopped coriander and parsley. Season to taste and cook for 1 minute, stirring to combine.

Transfer the lamb mixture to a sieve and drain to remove the fat. Put the mixture in a bowl and allow to cool slightly. Mix in the egg.

Count out six sheets of filo pastry (if the pastry is shorter than 39 cm (15½ in) in length, you will need extra sheets). Stack the filo on a cutting surface and, with a ruler and sharp knife, measure and cut across the width through the stack to give strips 12–13 cm (4½–5 in) wide and 28–30 cm (11¼–12 in) long. You will need 24 strips in total. Stack the cut filo in the folds of a damp tea towel (dish towel) or cover with plastic wrap to prevent it from drying out.

Place a strip of filo on the work surface with the narrow end towards you and brush with warm, melted butter. Top with another strip and brush the top with melted butter. Place 1 tablespoon of the filling 1 cm (½ in) in from the base and sides of the strip. Fold the end of the filo over the filling, fold in the sides and roll to the end of the strip. Place on a greased baking tray, seam side down. Repeat with the remaining ingredients. Brush the rolls with melted butter and sprinkle with sesame seeds.

Preheat the oven to 180°C (350°F/Gas 4). It is best to do this after the rolls are completed so that the kitchen remains cool during shaping. Bake the briouats for 15 minutes, or until lightly golden. Serve hot.

750 g (1 lb 10 oz) boneless lamb from leg
1 onion, grated
1 teaspoon paprika
1 teaspoon ground cumin
2 tablespoons finely chopped flat-leaf
    (Italian) parsley
3 tablespoons olive oil
1 round of Moroccan bread (page 114)
    or pitta breads, to serve

HARISSA AND TOMATO SAUCE
2 tomatoes
½ onion, grated
1 tablespoon olive oil
1 teaspoon harissa (page 250), or to
    taste, or ¼ teaspoon cayenne pepper
½ teaspoon sugar

Serves 4

Soak eight bamboo skewers in water for 2 hours, or use metal skewers.

Do not trim the fat from the lamb. Cut the meat into 3 cm (1¼ in) cubes and put in a bowl. Add the onion, paprika, cumin, parsley, olive oil and a generous grind of black pepper. Toss well to coat the lamb with the marinade, then cover and leave in the refrigerator to marinate for at least 2 hours.

To make the harissa and tomato sauce, halve the tomatoes crossways and squeeze out the seeds. Coarsely grate the tomatoes into a bowl down to the skin, discarding the skin. In a saucepan, cook the onion in the olive oil for 2 minutes, stir in the harissa or cayenne pepper, and add the grated tomatoes, sugar and ½ teaspoon salt. Cover and simmer for 10 minutes, then remove the lid and simmer for a further 4 minutes, or until the sauce reaches a thick, pouring consistency. Transfer to a bowl.

Thread the lamb cubes onto the skewers, leaving a little space between the meat cubes. Heat the barbecue grill to high and cook for 5–6 minutes, turning and brushing with the marinade. Alternatively, cook in a chargrill pan or under the grill (broiler).

If serving the kebabs with Moroccan bread, cut the bread into quarters and slit each piece in half almost to the crust. Slide the meat from the skewers into the bread pocket and drizzle with a little of the tomato and harissa sauce. If using pitta bread, do not split it; just slide the lamb from the skewers onto the centre, add the sauce and fold up the sides.

lamb kebabs

quenching the thirst...
With the Koran forbidding the consumption of alcohol, Muslims through the ages have found other beverages with which to express their hospitality. In Arabian countries, it is coffee; and in Morocco, it is mint tea, *na'na'* (which merits separate discussion, page 224) or other beverages to quench the thirst.

Flamboyant water sellers in city streets seem to validate the importance of this life-sustaining liquid. Wearing large-brimmed multicoloured hats festooned with tassels, their colourfully clad bodies gleam with polished brass — studded leather straps with clips for dangling chains, water cups and a bell — and a leather water

bag, reminiscent of the wineskin of Spain, slung around the waist. To tourists they are a glittering photo opportunity; to locals they are part of their traditions.

Introduced from Arabia many centuries ago is water flavoured with fragrant fumes. Grains of gum arabic are thrown on the embers of a charcoal brazier, and a pottery jug is inverted over the fragrant smoke until the pottery is impregnated with the fumes. Water is poured in, and as the water cools by evaporation the fragrance is absorbed.

At street stalls, from trolleys and in cafés, fresh fruit juices were popular long before they were embraced by the health-conscious elsewhere. Brilliant pyramids of oranges point the thirsty in the direction of orange juice sellers, where the juice is freshly squeezed and mixed with a drop of orange flower water, sugar for the sweet-

toothed, and perhaps a light dusting of cinnamon. Grape, pomegranate and watermelon juice; and *sharbat*, a drink of fruit or nuts, blended with milk or buttermilk — all are perfect thirst-quenchers.

The French left their legacy of viniculture and viticulture, and although the acreage of vineyards has been considerably reduced since Morocco regained its independence from France in 1956, Moroccan wines are still produced. The main growing areas are near the cities of Rabat and Casablanca on the Atlantic coast, and in the Atlas Mountain foothills around Meknes and Fez. Satisfactory white wines, and good red and rosé wines are produced, with much of the red wine exported for blending. Two brands of beer are also brewed under licence.

h◦t chickpeas

220 g (7¾ oz / 1 cup) dried chickpeas or
  2 x 420 g (15 oz) tins chickpeas
2 tablespoons olive oil
1 onion, finely chopped
1 small green capsicum (pepper), chopped
1 teaspoon ground cumin
2 tablespoons finely chopped coriander
  (cilantro) leaves

Serves 4–6

To cook dried chickpeas, first soak them overnight in three times their volume of cold water. Drain and place in a saucepan with fresh water to cover and simmer gently for 1 hour, or until tender, adding salt to taste towards the end of cooking. Drain, reserving 250 ml (9 fl oz / 1 cup) of the cooking liquid.

If using tinned chickpeas, drain them, reserving 250 ml (9 fl oz / 1 cup) of the liquid.

Warm the olive oil in a saucepan over medium heat. Add the onion and cook until lightly golden, then add the capsicum, cumin and coriander and cook for a few seconds. Add the chickpeas and their liquid, and freshly ground black pepper, to taste. Bring to a simmer, cover and simmer until heated through.

Adjust the seasoning and serve hot in small bowls with bread. As street food, chickpeas are drained of liquid and served in paper cones.

1 small onion, roughly chopped
2 tablespoons chopped flat-leaf (Italian)
  parsley
1 tablespoon chopped coriander
  (cilantro) leaves
500 g (1 lb 2 oz) minced (ground)
  lamb or beef
1 teaspoon ground cumin
1 teaspoon paprika
¼ teaspoon cayenne pepper
¼ teaspoon freshly ground black pepper
lemon wedges, to serve

Serves 4

Put the onion, parsley and coriander in the bowl of a food processor and process to a purée. Add the lamb, cumin, paprika, cayenne pepper, black pepper and 1 teaspoon salt. Process to a paste, scraping down the side of the bowl occasionally.

Divide the kefta mixture into eight even portions. Moisten your hands with water and mould each portion into a sausage shape about 9 cm (3½ in) long. Insert a flat metal skewer through the centre of each kefta sausage. Place on a tray, cover with plastic wrap and chill for 1 hour.

Cook on a hot barbecue grill or in a chargrill pan, turning frequently to brown evenly. The kefta are cooked until they are just well done (about 10 minutes)—they will feel firm when pressed lightly with tongs.

Serve the keftas with lemon wedges and salad greens. If desired, provide separate small dishes of ground cumin and salt, to be added according to individual taste.

kefta kebabs

merguez with capsicum and onion

8 merguez sausages
1 green capsicum (pepper)
1 red capsicum (pepper)
1 large onion
2 tablespoons olive oil
2 rounds of Moroccan bread (page 114)
   or pitta breads, to serve

Serves 4

Prick the sausages with a fork, then cook them on a barbecue grill over low–medium heat, turning frequently, for 8–10 minutes, or until cooked through. Alternatively, cook the sausages in a chargrill pan.

Meanwhile, cut the capsicums into quarters, remove the seeds and white membrane and cut into strips about 1 cm (½ in) wide. Halve the onion and slice thinly. Heat the olive oil in a frying pan on the barbecue, add the capsicum strips and onion and cook over medium heat, stirring often, for about 10 minutes, or until tender. If the onion begins to burn, reduce the heat to low or move the pan to a cooler section of the barbecue. Season with salt and freshly ground black pepper.

If serving with Moroccan bread, cut the rounds into quarters. Place the sausages and a generous amount of the capsicum and onion mixture in the bread, or roll up in pitta bread. Alternatively, serve the sausages on plates with the vegetables, and the bread on the side.

500 g (1 lb 2 oz) lamb liver in one piece
1 teaspoon paprika
½ teaspoon ground cumin
¼ teaspoon cayenne pepper
2 tablespoons olive oil
1 round of Moroccan bread (page 114)
  or pitta breads, to serve
ground cumin, coarse salt and cayenne
  pepper, or 60 g (2¼ oz/¼ cup) harissa
  (page 250), to serve

Serves 4

Soak eight bamboo skewers in water for 2 hours, or use metal skewers.

Pull off the fine membrane covering the liver. Cut the liver into 2 cm (¾ in) slices, then cut into cubes, removing any tubes from the liver as necessary. Put in a bowl and sprinkle with the paprika, cumin, cayenne pepper and 1 teaspoon salt. Add the olive oil and toss well. Set aside for 5 minutes.

Thread five or six pieces of liver onto the skewers, leaving a little space between the pieces. Cook on a barbecue grill or in a chargrill pan, brushing with any of the oil remaining in the bowl. Cook for about 1 minute each side—the liver should remain pink in the centre, otherwise it will toughen.

If using Moroccan bread for the liver kebabs, cut the bread into quarters and slit each piece in half almost to the crust. For each serve, slide the liver from two skewers into the bread pocket. If using pitta bread, do not split it; just slide the liver from the skewers onto the centre and fold up the sides. Offer small separate dishes of ground cumin, coarse salt and cayenne pepper to be added to taste. If using harissa, stir 3 tablespoons hot water into the harissa and serve as a sauce.

liver kebabs

the spice shop... The Arabs had been involved in the spice trade for centuries before their armies marched forth from Arabia to spread the teachings of the Prophet. When they reached Morocco in the late seventh century, they brought their spices with them and these have been part of the Moroccan kitchen ever since.

In the spice shops of the *souks*, the ground spices — reds, yellows and all shades of brown — are mounded and smoothed in baskets, bins, bowls or bags.

Whole spices — buds, bark, quills, nutmegs and cardamom pods, tears of gum arabic, dried chillies and fragrant rosebuds — contrast with the smooth mounds of the ground spices. The mingling aromas give a promise of what they can do to uplift the next meal to be cooked. The eight important spices for Moroccan cooking are cinnamon, cumin, saffron (sold in small, clear plastic containers to maintain freshness), paprika, turmeric, black pepper, *fefla soudaniya* (similar to cayenne pepper) and ginger. Then there are cloves, allspice, coriander seeds, fenugreek, aniseed and caraway seeds. As tempting as the aromas might be, Moroccan cooks only purchase spices in small amounts to ensure freshness, taking their purchases home in twisted paper packages to be stored in pottery jars in their kitchens.

Each spice shop has its own *ras el hanout*, which translates as 'top of the shop' or 'shopkeeper's choice'. This mixture may contain as few as 10 or as many as 26 different ground spices, depending on the whim of the shopkeeper. Spices may include pepper, cayenne pepper, lavender, thyme, rosemary, cumin, ginger, allspice, nutmeg, mace, cardamom, cloves, cinnamon, fenugreek and grains of paradise, also known as melegueta pepper. Orris root, cubeb pepper, belladonna, rosebuds, hashish and other ingredients, some not available outside Morocco, might be included, depending, of course, on the shopkeeper.

moroccan doughnuts

2 teaspoons active dried yeast
½ teaspoon sugar
310 g (11 oz/2½ cups) plain (all-purpose)
 flour
oil, for deep-frying
caster (superfine) sugar, to serve
ground cinnamon, to serve (optional)

Makes 20

Dissolve the yeast in 125 ml (4 fl oz/½ cup) of lukewarm water and stir in the sugar. Mix the flour and ½ teaspoon salt in a shallow mixing bowl and make a well in the centre. Pour the yeast mixture into the well and add a further 125 ml (4 fl oz/½ cup) of lukewarm water. Stir sufficient flour into the liquid to form a thin batter, cover the bowl with a cloth and leave for 15 minutes until bubbles form. Gradually stir in the remaining flour, then mix with your hand to form a soft dough. If too stiff, add a little more water, 1 teaspoon at a time. Knead for 5 minutes in the bowl until smooth and elastic. Pour a little oil down the side of the bowl, turn the dough to coat in the oil, cover and leave for 1 hour until doubled in bulk.

Punch down the dough, then turn it out onto the work surface and divide into 20 even-sized portions. With lightly oiled hands, roll each into a smooth ball. Brush a baking tray with oil. Using your index finger, punch a hole in the centre of one dough ball, then twirl it on your finger until the hole enlarges to 2 cm (¾ in) in diameter. Place on the tray. Repeat with the remaining balls.

Fill a large saucepan one-third full of oil and heat to 190°C (375°F), or until a cube of bread dropped in the oil browns in 10 seconds. Have a long metal skewer on hand and begin with the first doughnut that was shaped. Drop the doughnut into the oil, immediately put the skewer in the centre, and twirl it around in a circular motion for 2–3 seconds to keep the hole open. Fry for 1½–2 minutes, or until the doughnut is evenly browned. Once this process is mastered, drop 2–3 doughnuts at a time into the oil, briefly twirling the skewer in the centre of the first before adding the next. When cooked, put the skewer in the doughnut hole and lift it out onto a tray lined with paper towels.

Toss the doughnuts in caster sugar and eat while hot with coffee or mint tea. While it is not traditional in Morocco, cinnamon may be mixed with the sugar.

800 g (1 lb 12 oz) watermelon
1 teaspoon rosewater

Serves 2

Chill the watermelon thoroughly. Remove the rind and cut the pink part only into thick chunks that will fit into the juice extractor feed tube. Extract the juice into a pitcher. Take care when extracting the juice, as the seeds have a tendency to jump out of the feed tube.

Add the rosewater and pour into two tall glasses, or store the juice in the refrigerator until ready to serve.

watermelon juice with rosewater

orange juice with orange flower water

6 sweet oranges
caster (superfine) sugar, to taste
1½ teaspoons orange flower water
ground cinnamon, to serve (optional)

Serves 2

Choose sweet oranges and store them in the refrigerator so they are well chilled. Using a citrus juicer, juice the oranges, then pour the juice through a sieve into a pitcher.

Stir in the caster sugar, to taste (you may not need to add any sugar if the oranges are very sweet), and add the orange flower water. Pour into two tall glasses and lightly dust the top with cinnamon, if desired. Serve immediately.

500 g (1 lb 2 oz) chilled black grapes,
   seedless if possible
1 teaspoon rosewater
ground cinnamon, to serve (optional)

Serves 2

Wash the grapes very well, drain them, then cut off the thicker stalks, leaving the grapes in little bunches. Feed the grapes into the juice extractor, catching the juice in a pitcher. When the grapes are juiced, let the juice settle and then skim off any dark froth (this is the remnants of the stems and seeds). Cover the pitcher with plastic wrap and chill in the refrigerator for at least 1 hour.

Decant the juice into two tall glasses, leaving any sediment in the pitcher. Stir ½ teaspoon rosewater into each glass and dust the top lightly with cinnamon, if desired.

grape juice with rosewater

a little taste of...

In most Moroccan villages, the day begins by making the bread. Traditionally, it is the women of the household who do the cooking and make the bread, once or twice each day. The bread is shaped and left to rise. On their way to school, the children carry the uncooked loaves to the communal bakery; they collect the bread on their way home at midday. The midday meal is the main meal, which usually begins with two or three salads, their content dictated by the season, followed by a tagine, or stew. To prepare the tagine, grated onion, garlic, herbs and spices are mixed with olive oil, which is rubbed into pieces of lamb, beef or chicken and left to marinate. The tagine is then placed over a charcoal fire to simmer slowly. With these traditional cooking methods and using the most basic kitchen equipment, the women of Morocco have developed an interesting and varied cuisine — yet they are open to change. While many households prefer to use charcoal fires for cooking, in others, the food may be cooked using a *mijotte*, a pressure cooker, and bottled gas.

...home cooking

broad bean dip

**185 g (6½ oz/1 cup) dried broad
(fava) beans or ready-skinned
dried broad beans**
2 garlic cloves, crushed
½ teaspoon ground cumin
1½ tablespoons lemon juice
up to 80 ml (2½ fl oz/⅓ cup) olive oil
a large pinch of paprika
**2 tablespoons chopped flat-leaf
(Italian) parsley**
flat bread, to serve

Serves 6

Put the dried broad beans in a large bowl, cover with 500 ml (17 fl oz/ 2 cups) cold water and leave to soak. If using dried beans with skins, soak them for 24 hours, changing the water once. If using ready-skinned dried beans, soak them for 12 hours only.

Drain the beans. If using beans with skins, remove the skins. To do this, slit the skin with the point of a knife and slip the bean out of its skin.

Put the beans in a large saucepan with water to cover and bring to the boil. Cover and simmer over low heat for 1 hour, or until tender (if the water boils over, uncover the pan a little). After 1 hour, remove the lid and cook for a further 15 minutes, or until most of the liquid has evaporated, taking care that the beans do not catch on the base of the pan.

Purée the beans in a food processsor, then transfer to a bowl and stir in the garlic, cumin and lemon juice. Add salt, to taste. Gradually stir in enough olive oil to give a spreadable or thick dipping consistency, starting with half the oil. As the mixture cools it may become thicker, in which case you can stir through a little warm water to return the mixture to a softer consistency.

Spread the bean purée over a large dish and sprinkle the paprika and parsley over the top. Serve with flat bread.

1.5 kg (3 lb 5 oz) ripe tomatoes
3 tablespoons olive oil
2 onions, coarsely grated
2 garlic cloves, crushed
1 teaspoon ground ginger
1 cinnamon stick
¼ teaspoon freshly ground black pepper
¼ teaspoon ground saffron threads
   (optional)
3 tablespoons tomato paste
   (concentrated purée)
2 tablespoons honey
1½ teaspoons ground cinnamon

Makes 625 ml (21½ fl oz/2½ cups)

Halve the tomatoes crossways, then squeeze out the seeds. Coarsely grate the tomatoes into a bowl down to the skin, discarding the skin. Set aside.

Heat the olive oil in a heavy-based saucepan over low heat and add the onion. Cook for 5 minutes, then stir in the garlic, ginger, cinnamon stick and pepper and cook for about 1 minute. Add the saffron, if using, the tomato paste and grated tomatoes and season with ½ teaspoon salt.

Simmer, uncovered, over medium heat for 45–50 minutes, or until most of the liquid evaporates, stirring often when the sauce starts to thicken to prevent it catching on the base of the pan. When the oil begins to separate, stir in the honey and cinnamon and cook over low heat for 2 minutes. Adjust the seasoning with salt if necessary.

Serve with other salads in the traditional Moroccan way—eaten with bread at the beginning of a meal. In Morocco, this is also used as a basis for some tagines (lamb tagine with sweet tomato jam, page 96), or as a stuffing for fish. Store in a clean, sealed jar in the refrigerator for up to 1 week.

sweet
tomato jam

the souks...

The *souks*, or markets, of Morocco are just one of the places from which Moroccans buy their foods, but these are by far the most fascinating, especially those located within the crumbling walls of the *medina*, the ancient Arab quarter.

Rows of small stalls, their tables piled high with the season's produce, provide a riot of magnificent colour — rich red tomatoes, a tumble of bright orange carrots, glossy green and red capsicums (peppers), purple eggplants (aubergines), red, golden and white onions, crisp white turnips, waxy green cucumbers and zucchini (courgettes), red and white radishes, and young green peas. Men sit in their stalls, offering wild artichokes, tender wild asparagus, fragrant strawberries, or freshly laid eggs from their woven baskets or wooden crates. Nearby, a trolley is laden with fresh coriander (cilantro), another with fragrant mint, and the smell of freshly baked bread wafts from a cloth-covered table of wooden crates. Open-fronted shops display an array of wonderful spices, for which Morocco is renowned, as well as a selection of olives and preserved lemons, fresh dates, figs, nuts and raisins, chickpeas and couscous, or slabs of nougat studded with almonds.

The stalls of the meat market are jammed too. Sides of lamb hang from the roof, some camel haunches are on offer, as well as cages with rabbits, chickens, ducks and pigeons. These are usually sold live, but the poultry seller will dispatch and pluck the birds on request.

Shoppers move purposefully, male shoppers bargaining for the best price. The haggling, the shouting, the braying of donkeys, the smell of kebabs cooking, the pervading aromas — especially of spices and mint — all combine to make shopping in the *souk* an unforgettable experience.

orange and radish salad

3 sweet oranges
12 red radishes
1 tablespoon lemon juice
2 teaspoons caster (superfine) sugar
2 tablespoons olive oil
1 tablespoon orange flower water
ground cinnamon, to serve
small mint leaves, to serve

Serves 4

Cut off the peel from the oranges using a sharp knife, removing all traces of pith and cutting through the outer membranes to expose the flesh. Holding the oranges over a small bowl to catch the juice, segment them by cutting between the membranes. Remove the seeds from the orange segments, then put the segments in the bowl. Squeeze the remains of the orange into the bowl.

Drain the orange segments, reserving the orange juice, and return the drained oranges to the bowl. Set the juice aside.

Wash the radishes and trim off the roots. Slice thinly using a mandolin or vegetable slicer. Add to the orange segments.

Put 2 tablespoons of the reserved orange juice in a small bowl, add the lemon juice, sugar, olive oil and a pinch of salt. Beat well and pour over the salad. Sprinkle with orange flower water, toss lightly, then cover and chill for 15 minutes. Transfer to a serving bowl, sprinkle the top lightly with cinnamon and scatter with the mint leaves.

2 green capsicums (peppers)
4 tomatoes
1 red onion
1 garlic clove, finely chopped
1 tablespoon finely chopped flat-leaf
  (Italian) parsley
80 ml (2½ fl oz/⅓ cup) olive oil
1 tablespoon red wine vinegar

Serves 4

Cut the capsicums into large flattish pieces and remove the seeds and white membranes. Place the pieces, skin side up, under a grill (broiler) and grill (broil) until the skin blackens. Turn them over and cook for 2–3 minutes on the fleshy side. Remove the cooked capsicum and place in a plastic bag, tuck the end of the bag underneath and leave to steam in the bag until cool enough to handle. Remove the blackened skin and cut into short strips. Place in a bowl.

Peel the tomatoes. To do this, score a cross in the base of each one using a knife. Put the tomatoes in a bowl of boiling water for 20 seconds, then plunge into a bowl of cold water to cool. Remove from the water and peel the skin away from the cross—it should slip off easily. Cut the tomatoes in half crossways and squeeze out the seeds. Dice the tomatoes and add to the capsicum. Halve the onion lengthways and remove the root. Cut into slender wedges. Add to the bowl, along with the garlic and parsley.

Beat the olive oil with the red wine vinegar and add ½ teaspoon salt and a good grinding of black pepper. Pour the dressing over the salad ingredients and toss well.

tomato, onion and capsicum salad

beetroot and cumin salad

6 beetroot (beets)
80 ml (2½ fl oz / ⅓ cup) olive oil
1 tablespoon red wine vinegar
½ teaspoon ground cumin
1 red onion
2 tablespoons chopped flat-leaf
  (Italian) parsley

Serves 4–6

Cut the stems from the beetroot bulbs, leaving 2 cm (¾ in) attached. Do not trim the roots. Wash well to remove all traces of soil, and boil in salted water for 1 hour, or until tender. Leave until cool enough to handle.

In a deep bowl, beat the olive oil with the red wine vinegar, cumin and a good grinding of black pepper to make a dressing.

Wearing rubber gloves so the beetroot juice doesn't stain your hands, peel the warm beetroot bulbs and trim the roots. Halve them and cut into slender wedges and place in the dressing. Halve the onion, slice into slender wedges and add to the beetroot. Add the parsley and toss well. Serve this salad warm or at room temperature.

3 tablespoons olive oil
1 onion, chopped
2 garlic cloves, crushed
500 g (1 lb 2 oz) fresh okra, or 800 g
   (1 lb 12 oz) tinned okra, rinsed and
   drained
400 g (14 oz) tin chopped tomatoes
2 teaspoons sugar
3 tablespoons lemon juice
3 large handfuls coriander (cilantro)
   leaves, finely chopped

Serves 4–6

Heat the oil in a large frying pan over medium heat, add the onion and cook for 5 minutes, or until the onion is transparent and golden. Add the garlic and cook for another minute.

If using fresh okra, add it to the pan and cook, stirring, for 4–5 minutes. Add the tomatoes, sugar and lemon juice and simmer, stirring occasionally, for 3–4 minutes. Stir in the coriander (and the tinned okra, if you are using it), remove from the heat and serve.

okra with tomato sauce

eggplant jam

2 eggplants (aubergines), about 400 g
  (14 oz), cut into 1 cm (½ in) thick slices
olive oil, for frying
2 garlic cloves, crushed
1 teaspoon paprika
1½ teaspoons ground cumin
2 tablespoons chopped coriander
  (cilantro) leaves
½ teaspoon sugar
1 tablespoon lemon juice

Serves 6–8

Sprinkle the eggplant slices with salt and drain in a colander for 30 minutes. Rinse well, squeeze gently and pat dry. Heat about 5 mm (¼ in) of the oil in a large frying pan over medium heat and fry the eggplant in batches until golden brown on both sides. Drain on paper towels, then chop finely.

Put the eggplant in a colander and leave it until most of the oil has drained off, then transfer to a bowl and add the garlic, paprika, cumin, coriander and sugar.

Wipe out the pan, add the eggplant mixture and stir constantly over medium heat for 2 minutes. Transfer to a bowl, stir in the lemon juice and season with salt and pepper. Serve at room temperature. Serve with bread as a dip, or with other salads.

4 Lebanese (short) cucumbers
1 red onion
3 teaspoons caster (superfine) sugar
1 tablespoon red wine vinegar
3 tablespoons olive oil
½ teaspoon finely crumbled dried za'atar
**   or 1 teaspoon finely chopped lemon**
**   thyme**
90 g (3¼ oz/½ cup) black olives
flat bread, to serve

Serves 4

Wash the cucumbers and dry with paper towels. Do not peel the cucumbers if the skins are tender. Coarsely grate the cucumbers, mix the grated flesh with ½ teaspoon salt and leave to drain well.

Halve the onion and chop it finely. Add to the cucumber, along with the sugar and toss together.

In a small bowl, beat the red wine vinegar with the olive oil, then add the za'atar or lemon thyme, and freshly ground black pepper, to taste. Whisk the ingredients together and pour over the cucumber. Cover and chill for 15 minutes. Scatter with olives and serve with flat bread.

cucumber and olive salad

marinated olives

PRESERVED LEMON OLIVES
½ preserved lemon (page 251)
½ teaspoon finely chopped red chilli
½ teaspoon ground cumin
2 tablespoons finely chopped coriander
    (cilantro) leaves
2 tablespoons finely chopped flat-leaf
    (Italian) parsley
2 garlic cloves, finely chopped
2 tablespoons lemon juice
125 ml (4 fl oz/½ cup) olive oil
500 g (1 lb 2 oz/3 cups) cured green
    olives (whole or cracked)

HARISSA OLIVES
1 red capsicum (pepper) or 2 tablespoons
    chopped roasted capsicum
2 teaspoons harissa (page 250)
2 garlic cloves, finely chopped
125 ml (4 fl oz/½ cup) olive oil
500 g (1 lb 2 oz/2⅔ cups) black olives,
    such as kalamata

Makes about 500 g (1 lb 2 oz/3 cups)

To make the preserved lemon olives, rinse the preserved lemon half under cold running water. Remove the pulp and membrane and rinse the rind. Drain and pat dry with paper towels. Chop the lemon rind very finely and put in a bowl, along with the chilli, cumin, coriander, parsley, garlic and lemon juice. Stir well and beat in the olive oil. Rinse the green olives under cold running water and drain thoroughly. Add to the preserved lemon marinade, toss and transfer to clean jars.

To make the harissa olives, first roast the capsicum (skip this step if you have ready-prepared roasted capsicum). Cut the capsicum into quarters, removing the seeds and white membrane. Have the pieces as flat as possible and place them, skin side up, under a hot grill (broiler) and grill (broil) until the skin blisters and blackens. Turn and cook for 2–3 minutes on the fleshy side. Place the pieces in a plastic bag, tuck the end of the bag underneath and steam for 15 minutes. Remove the blackened skin, rinse and drain the capsicum pieces, then pat dry with paper towels. Finely chop one of the pieces—you will need 2 tablespoons of chopped roasted capsicum. (Use the remaining roasted capsicum in salads.) In a bowl, combine the chopped capsicum with the harissa and garlic, then beat in the olive oil. Rinse the black olives under cold running water and drain thoroughly. Add to the harissa marinade, toss and transfer to clean jars.

Seal the jars and refrigerate for 1–2 days before using. Bring the olives to room temperature 1 hour before serving. Use the preserved lemon olives within 5 days; the harissa olives within 10 days.

**500 g (1 lb 2 oz) carrots, peeled and cut
into 6 x 1.5 cm (2½ x ⅝ in) sticks**
½ teaspoon paprika
½ teaspoon ground cumin
**2 tablespoons finely chopped flat-leaf
(Italian) parsley**
1 tablespoon lemon juice
2 tablespoons olive oil

Serves 4

Cook the carrots in boiling, salted water for 10 minutes, or until tender. Drain and toss lightly with the paprika, cumin, parsley, lemon juice and olive oil.

Place in a serving bowl, cover and leave in the refrigerator for 2 hours for the flavours to develop. Season with salt. Serve warm or at room temperature.

spiced carrots

preserved lemon and tomato salad

750 g (1 lb 10 oz) tomatoes
1 red onion
1 preserved lemon (page 251)
3 tablespoons olive oil
1 tablespoon lemon juice
½ teaspoon paprika
1 tablespoon finely chopped flat-leaf
   (Italian) parsley
2 tablespoons finely chopped coriander
   (cilantro) leaves

Serves 4

Peel the tomatoes. To do this, score a cross in the base of each one using a knife. Put the tomatoes in a bowl of boiling water for 20 seconds, then plunge them into a bowl of cold water to cool. Remove from the water and peel the skin away from the cross—it should slip off easily. Cut the tomatoes in half crossways and then squeeze out the seeds. Dice the tomatoes and put them in a bowl.

Halve the onion lengthways, cut out the root end, slice into slender wedges and add to the bowl.

Separate the preserved lemon into quarters, remove the pulp and membrane and discard them. Rinse the rind under cold running water, dry with paper towels and cut into strips. Add to the onion and tomato.

In a small bowl, beat the oil, lemon juice and paprika, and add ½ teaspoon salt and a good grinding of black pepper. Pour the dressing over the salad, toss lightly, then cover and set aside for 30 minutes. Just before serving, add the parsley and coriander and toss again. If preparing this salad ahead of time, cover the bowl and place in the refrigerator, but bring to room temperature before adding the chopped herbs.

bread... To a Moroccan, bread, or *khobz*, is sacred, to be revered, savoured and never wasted. *Kesra*, or country bread, is made every day in rural households, the dough mixed and kneaded in a shallow wooden or earthenware vessel called a *gsaa*. It is a simple bread, made with wholemeal (whole wheat) flour, usually mixed with unbleached flour, and perhaps a handful of yellow cornmeal or barley flour. Only water, a little salt and sugar are used in the dough,

which is leavened with a sourdough starter kept from the previous day's baking (though often supplemented with dried yeast granules these days).

Shaped in flattish round loaves and placed on trays, the loaves are stamped with each household's own mark for identification, covered with a cloth and left to rise only once. Anise seeds and sesame seeds are sometimes used to flavour the bread, or are sprinkled over the top. The loaves are then taken on trays to the local bakery or baked in a communal oven — the marking on each loaf clearly identifying the owner.

These flattish loaves have a loose crumb that can absorb the sauce of the tagine, but are still crusty enough to support food as it is conveyed to the mouth with the fingers. The bread is cut into wedges and distributed by one person at the table — to prevent household quarrels. Flatter loaves are made for eating with kebabs, and baguettes, a legacy from the French, are baked in some bakeries and patisseries.

Other breads of the *bled*, countryside, include a bread sheet called *therfist*, which is cooked on a pottery dome over embers. Another, made by the Tuaregs, the nomadic Berbers of the Sahara, is called *tagella* and is cooked on hot stones.

60 g (2¼ oz) butter
1 large onion, finely chopped
2 garlic cloves, finely chopped
1 teaspoon ground ginger
1 teaspoon ground turmeric
1 cinnamon stick
pinch of cayenne pepper, or ½ teaspoon
    harissa (page 250), or to taste
500 ml (17 fl oz/2 cups) vegetable
    or chicken stock
⅛ teaspoon ground saffron threads
600 g (1 lb 5 oz) butternut pumpkin
    (squash) or other firm pumpkin,
    peeled and cubed
500 g (1 lb 2 oz) orange sweet potato,
    peeled and cubed
60 g (2¼ oz/½ cup) raisins
1 tablespoon honey
coriander (cilantro) leaves, to serve

Serves 4–6

Melt the butter in a large saucepan over low heat. Add the onion and cook gently, stirring occasionally, until softened. Add the garlic, ginger, turmeric, cinnamon stick and the cayenne pepper or harissa. Stir over low heat for 1–2 minutes. Pour in the stock, add the saffron, then increase the heat to medium and bring to the boil.

Add the pumpkin, sweet potato, raisins and honey and season with salt and freshly ground black pepper. Cover and simmer for a further 15 minutes, or until the vegetables are tender. Remove the cinnamon stick, transfer to a bowl and scatter with coriander leaves.

Stews such as this are traditionally served as a hot or warm vegetable course after the appetizer salads, but can be served as a vegetable accompaniment to the main meal. This goes well with chicken.

pumpkin and sweet potato stew

tagine of chickpeas

3 tablespoons olive oil
1 onion, chopped
1 garlic clove, finely chopped
1 teaspoon harissa (page 250), or to
   taste, or ¼ teaspoon cayenne pepper
½ teaspoon paprika
¼ teaspoon ground ginger
½ teaspoon ground turmeric
1 teaspoon ground cumin
1 teaspoon ground cinnamon
400 g (14 oz) tin chopped tomatoes
1 teaspoon sugar
2 x 420 g (15 oz) tins chickpeas
3 tablespoons chopped flat-leaf
   (Italian) parsley
2 tablespoons chopped coriander
   (cilantro) leaves

Serves 4

Put the olive oil and onion in a large saucepan and cook over medium heat for 7–8 minutes, or until softened. Stir in the garlic, the harissa or cayenne pepper, and the spices and cook gently for 2 minutes. Add the tomatoes and sugar and season, to taste. Cover and simmer for 20 minutes.

Meanwhile, drain the chickpeas and put them in a large bowl with enough cold water to cover well. Lift up handfuls of chickpeas and rub them between your hands to loosen the skins. Run more water into the bowl, stir well and let the skins float to the top, then skim them off. Repeat until all the skins have been removed.

Drain the chickpeas again and stir them into the tomato mixture. Cover and simmer for 20–25 minutes, adding a little more water if necessary. Stir through the parsley and coriander and season, to taste. Serve with crusty bread or with couscous.

700 g (1 lb 9 oz) minced (ground) lamb
1 small onion, finely chopped
2 garlic cloves, finely chopped
2 tablespoons finely chopped flat-leaf
   (Italian) parsley
2 tablespoons finely chopped coriander
   (cilantro) leaves
½ teaspoon cayenne pepper
½ teaspoon ground ginger
1 teaspoon ground cumin
1 teaspoon paprika
2 tablespoons olive oil
4 eggs

SAUCE
2 tablespoons olive oil
1 onion, finely chopped
2 garlic cloves, finely chopped
2 teaspoons ground cumin
½ teaspoon ground cinnamon
1 teaspoon paprika
2 x 400 g (14 oz) tins chopped tomatoes
2 teaspoons harissa (page 250),
   or to taste
4 tablespoons chopped coriander
   (cilantro) leaves

Serves 4

Put the lamb, onion, garlic, herbs and spices in a bowl and mix well. Season with salt and pepper. Roll tablespoons of the mixture into balls.

Heat the oil in a large frying pan over medium–high heat, add the meatballs in batches and cook for 8–10 minutes, turning occasionally, or until browned all over. Remove the meatballs and set them aside in a bowl. Wipe the frying pan with paper towels.

To make the sauce, heat the olive oil in the frying pan, add the onion and cook over medium heat for 5 minutes, or until the onion is soft. Add the garlic, cumin, cinnamon and paprika and cook for 1 minute, or until fragrant. Stir in the tomatoes and harissa and bring to the boil. Reduce the heat and simmer for 20 minutes.

Add the meatballs, cover and simmer for 10 minutes, or until cooked. Stir in the coriander, then carefully break the eggs into the simmering tagine and cook until just set. Season and serve with crusty bread to mop up the juices.

kefta tagine

slow-cooked
beef with herbs

1 kg (2 lb 4 oz) chuck steak or
    boneless beef shin
1½ onions, finely chopped
4 garlic cloves, finely chopped
2 tablespoons olive oil
2 teaspoons ras el hanout (page 250)
½ teaspoon harissa (page 250), or to
    taste, or ⅛ teaspoon cayenne pepper
¼ teaspoon freshly ground black pepper
3 ripe tomatoes
1½ preserved lemons (page 251)
2 teaspoons honey
1 tablespoon chopped coriander
    (cilantro) leaves
2 tablespoons chopped flat-leaf
    (Italian) parsley

Serves 4–6

Trim the beef and cut into 2.5 cm (1 in) pieces. Place the beef in a deep casserole dish. Add the onion, garlic, oil, ras el hanout, harissa or cayenne pepper, the black pepper and season with salt. Toss the meat with the marinade. Preheat the oven to 140°C (275°F/Gas 1).

Halve the tomatoes crossways and squeeze out the seeds. Coarsely grate the tomatoes down to the skins, grating them straight into the casserole. Discard the skins. Rinse the preserved lemons and remove the pulp and membranes. Chop the rind into chunks, reserving some for garnish, and add to the meat, along with the honey, coriander and 1 tablespoon of the parsley. Stir well, then cover and cook in the oven for 3½ hours. Juices from the meat should keep the dish moist, but check after 1½ hours of cooking and add a little water if necessary.

When the meat is very tender, transfer to a serving dish, scatter over the reserved lemon rind and garnish with the remaining parsley.

4 lamb shanks, frenched
1 tablespoon oil
30 g (1 oz) butter
1 onion, chopped
¼ teaspoon ground saffron threads
½ teaspoon ground ginger
2 cinnamon sticks
4 coriander (cilantro) sprigs, tied in
   a bunch
zest of ½ lemon, removed in wide strips
300 g (10½ oz/1⅓ cups) pitted prunes
2 tablespoons honey
1 tablespoon sesame seeds, toasted

Serves 4

Frenched lamb shanks are trimmed of excess fat with the knuckle end of the bone sawn off. If unavailable, use whole shanks and ask the butcher to saw them in half for you.

Place a heavy-based saucepan over high heat, add the oil and butter, then add the lamb shanks. Brown the shanks on all sides and remove to a plate.

Reduce the heat to medium, add the onion and cook gently for 5 minutes to soften. Add 375 ml (13 fl oz/1½ cups) water, the saffron, ginger, cinnamon sticks and coriander sprigs and season, to taste. Stir well and return the lamb shanks to the pan. Cover and simmer over low heat for 1 hour, then add the strips of lemon zest and cook for a further 30 minutes.

Add the prunes and honey, cover and simmer for a further 30 minutes, or until the lamb is very tender. Remove and discard the coriander sprigs. Serve hot, sprinkled with sesame seeds.

lamb shank and prune tagine

chicken and quince tagine

1.5 kg (3 lb 5 oz) chicken, quartered
2 teaspoons ras el hanout (page 250)
2 tablespoons oil
1 onion, sliced
250 ml (9 fl oz/1 cup) chicken stock
90 g (3¼ oz) quince paste
1 tablespoon lemon juice
2 teaspoons rosewater

Serves 4

Cut diagonal slashes in the fleshy parts of the chicken pieces, such as the breasts, legs and thighs. Rub the ras el hanout into the chicken, cover and leave for 20 minutes to marinate.

Heat the oil in a large frying pan over medium heat. Add the chicken pieces in batches, skin side down, and brown lightly for 2 minutes, then turn them over and cook for a further 2 minutes. Remove to a plate.

Add the onion to the pan and cook for 5 minutes, or until soft. Add the stock, stir well to lift the browned juices off the base of the pan, then return the chicken to the pan. Season lightly with salt if necessary. Reduce the heat to low, then cover and simmer for 45 minutes, turning the chicken occasionally.

When the chicken is tender, cut the quince paste into thin slices, then add it to the pan juices, mashing it with a fork until it melts into the liquid. Stir in the lemon juice and rosewater and simmer for 1 minute. Serve the chicken with the quince sauce and spiced carrots (page 62).

1 kg (2 lb 4 oz) lamb shoulder, boned
3 tablespoons olive oil
2 onions, quartered
2 garlic cloves, finely chopped
½ teaspoon ground turmeric
½ teaspoon paprika
¼ teaspoon ground saffron threads
1 cinnamon stick
4 coriander (cilantro) sprigs and 4 flat-leaf
    (Italian) parsley sprigs, tied in a bunch
400 g (14 oz) tin chopped tomatoes
1½ teaspoons freshly ground black pepper
3 carrots, peeled and cut into thick sticks
3 small turnips, peeled and quartered

30 g (1 oz/¼ cup) raisins
4 zucchini (courgettes), cut into sticks
400 g (14 oz) firm pumpkin (winter
    squash) or butternut pumpkin (squash),
    peeled and cut into 2.5 cm (1 in) chunks
420 g (15 oz) tin chickpeas, rinsed and
    drained
1 quantity couscous (pages 248–9)
2–3 teaspoons harissa (page 250),
    to taste

Serves 6–8

Trim the lamb of excess fat if necessary, then cut into 2 cm (¾ in) cubes.

Heat the oil in a large saucepan or the base of a large couscoussier and add the lamb, onion and garlic. Cook over medium heat, turning the lamb once, just until the lamb loses its red colour. Stir in the turmeric, paprika and saffron, add 750 ml (26 fl oz/3 cups) water, then add the cinnamon stick, the bunch of herbs, tomatoes, pepper and 1½ teaspoons salt, or to taste. Bring to a gentle boil, then cover and simmer over low heat for 1 hour. Add the carrots and turnips and cook for a further 20 minutes.

Add the raisins, zucchini, pumpkin and chickpeas to the saucepan, adding a little water if necessary to almost cover the ingredients. Cook for a further 20 minutes, or until the meat and vegetables are tender.

While the stew is cooking, prepare the couscous. Steam it either over the stew or over a saucepan of boiling water, or in the microwave oven.

Pile the couscous in a deep, heated platter and make a dent in the centre. Remove the herbs and cinnamon stick from the stew and ladle the meat and vegetables on top of the couscous, letting some tumble down the sides. Moisten with a little broth from the stew. Pour 250 ml (9 fl oz/1 cup) of the remaining broth into a bowl and stir in the harissa. The harissa-flavoured broth is added to the couscous to keep it moist, and according to individual taste.

couscous with lamb and seven vegetables

spiced grilled chicken

2 x 750 g (1 lb 10 oz) chickens
a pinch of saffron threads
1 teaspoon coarse salt
2 garlic cloves, chopped
1½ teaspoons paprika
¼ teaspoon cayenne pepper
2 teaspoons ground cumin
½ teaspoon freshly ground black pepper

1 tablespoon lemon juice
1 tablespoon olive oil
2 lemons
2 tablespoons icing (confectioners')
  sugar
watercress, picked over, to serve

Serves 4

To prepare the chickens, cut them on each side of the backbone using poultry shears or kitchen scissors. Rinse the chickens and dry with paper towels. Open out on a board, skin side up, and press down with the heel of your hand on the top of each breast to break the breastbone and to flatten it. Cut deep slashes diagonally in each breast and on the legs. Using two long metal skewers for each chicken, push the skewers from the tip of each breast through to the underside of the legs, which should be spread outwards so that the thickness of the chicken is as even as possible.

Put the saffron in a mortar with the salt and pound with a pestle to pulverize the threads. Add the garlic and pound to a paste. Work in the paprika, cayenne pepper, cumin, black pepper, lemon juice and olive oil. Rub the spice mix into the chickens, rubbing it into the slashes. Cover and marinate in the refrigerator for at least 2 hours, or overnight. Bring the chickens to room temperature 1 hour before cooking.

Prepare a charcoal fire or preheat the barbecue and place the chickens on the grill, skin side up. Cook over medium heat for 20 minutes, continually turning the chicken as it cooks and brushing with any remaining marinade. The chicken is cooked if the juices run clear when the thigh is pierced. Cooking time can be shortened on a barbecue if a roasting tin is inverted over the chickens to act as a mini oven—reduce the heat to low to prevent burning. Transfer the chickens to a platter, remove the skewers, cover with a foil tent and leave to rest for 5 minutes before cutting in half to serve.

Cut the lemons in half crossways, remove any seeds, then cut again into quarters. Sift the icing sugar onto a large plate. Dip the cut surfaces of the lemon quarters in the icing sugar and place on the barbecue hotplate. Cook briefly on the cut surfaces until golden and caramelized. Serve the chickens with the lemon quarters and watercress.

275 g (9¾ oz/1½ cups) brown lentils
2 tomatoes
600 g (1 lb 5 oz) firm pumpkin
 (wintersquash) or butternut pumpkin
 (squash)
3 tablespoons olive oil
1 onion, finely chopped
3 garlic cloves, finely chopped
½ teaspoon ground cumin
½ teaspoon ground turmeric
¼ teaspoon cayenne pepper, or 1 teaspoon
 harissa (page 250), or to taste

1 teaspoon paprika
3 teaspoons tomato paste
 (concentrated purée)
½ teaspoon sugar
1 tablespoon finely chopped flat-leaf
 (Italian) parsley
2 tablespoons chopped coriander
 (cilantro) leaves

Serves 4–6

Pick over the lentils and discard any damaged lentils and any stones. Put the lentils in a sieve and rinse under cold running water. Tip into a saucepan and add 1 litre (35 fl oz/4 cups) cold water. Bring to the boil, skim the surface if necessary, then cover and simmer over low heat for 20 minutes.

Meanwhile, halve the tomatoes crossways and squeeze out the seeds. Coarsely grate the tomatoes into a bowl down to the skin, discarding the skin. Set the grated tomato aside. Peel and seed the pumpkin and cut into 3 cm (1¼ in) dice. Set aside.

Heat the oil in a large saucepan over low heat, add the onion and cook until softened. Add the garlic, cook for a few seconds, then stir in the cumin, turmeric and cayenne pepper or harissa. Cook for 30 seconds, then add the paprika, grated tomato, tomato paste, sugar, half of the parsley and coriander, 1 teaspoon salt and freshly ground black pepper, to taste.

Add the lentils and the prepared pumpkin, stir well, then cover and simmer for about 20 minutes, or until the pumpkin and lentils are tender. Adjust the seasoning and transfer to a serving bowl. Sprinkle with the remaining parsley and coriander leaves and serve hot or warm with crusty bread.

spiced lentil and pumpkin tagine

tagine of lamb, olives and potatoes

1 kg (2 lb 4 oz) boneless lamb shoulder
3 tablespoons olive oil
2 onions, finely chopped
2 garlic cloves, finely chopped
1 teaspoon ground cumin
½ teaspoon ground ginger
½ teaspoon paprika
3 tablespoons chopped coriander
   (cilantro) leaves

3 tablespoons chopped flat-leaf
   (Italian) parsley
175 g (6 oz/1 cup) green olives
750 g (1 lb 10 oz) all-purpose potatoes
¼ teaspoon ground saffron threads
1 tablespoon olive oil, extra

Serves 4–6

Trim the lamb and cut it into 3 cm (1¼ in) pieces. Heat half the olive oil in a large saucepan over high heat and brown the lamb on each side in batches, removing to a dish when cooked. Add a little more oil as required.

Reduce the heat to low, add the remaining olive oil and cook the onion for 5 minutes, or until softened. Add the garlic, cumin and ginger and cook for a few seconds. Add 375 ml (13 fl oz/1½ cups) water and stir well to lift the browned juices off the base of the pan. Return the lamb to the pan, along with the paprika, ½ teaspoon salt and a good grinding of black pepper. Add the coriander and parsley, then cover and simmer over low heat for 1–1¼ hours.

Meanwhile, put the olives in a small saucepan, cover with water, then bring to the boil and cook for 5 minutes. Drain and repeat once more to sweeten the flavour. Add the drained olives to the lamb, cover and cook for a further 15–30 minutes, or until the lamb is tender.

Peel the potatoes and cut them into quarters. Put in a pan, cover with lightly salted water and add the saffron. Bring to the boil and cook for 10 minutes, or until tender. Drain and toss lightly with the extra olive oil.

Transfer the lamb and sauce to a serving dish, arrange the potatoes around the lamb and serve.

2 tablespoons finely chopped onion
2 teaspoons olive oil
3 anchovy fillets, finely chopped
95 g (3½ oz) tin tuna in brine
2 teaspoons capers, rinsed, drained
  and chopped
2 tablespoons finely chopped flat-leaf
  (Italian) parsley

oil, for frying
4 x 21 cm (8¼ in) square spring roll
  wrappers (egg roll skins)
1 egg white, lightly beaten
4 small eggs

Serves 2

In a small frying pan, gently cook the onion in the olive oil until softened. Add the anchovies and cook, stirring, until the anchovies have melted. Tip into a bowl. Drain the tuna well and put it in the bowl, then add the capers and parsley. Mix well, breaking up the chunks of tuna. Divide the mixture in the bowl into four portions.

Pour the oil into a large frying pan to a depth of 1 cm (½ in) and place over medium heat.

Put a spring roll wrapper on the work surface and brush around the edge with beaten egg white. Put a quarter of the filling on one corner of the wrapper, with the edge of the filling just touching the centre of the wrapper. Make an indent in the filling with the back of a spoon and break an egg into the centre of the filling. Fold the pastry over to form a triangle and firmly press the edges together to seal.

As soon as you have finished the first pastry triangle, carefully lift it up using a wide spatula to help support the filling, and slide it into the hot oil. Fry for about 30 seconds on each side, spooning hot oil on top at the beginning of frying. If a firmly cooked egg is preferred, cook for 50 seconds on each side. When golden brown and crisp, remove with the spatula and drain on paper towels. Repeat with the remaining wrappers and filling. Do not be tempted to prepare all the pastry triangles before frying them, as the moist filling soaks through the wrapper.

The traditional way to eat these is to hold it by the corners, with the filling side upwards, and bite into the egg, allowing the runny yolk to act as a sauce for the filling ingredients. Alternatively, use a knife and fork to eat them.

tuna brik

beef tagine with sweet potatoes

1 kg (2 lb 4 oz) blade or chuck steak
3 tablespoons olive oil
1 onion, finely chopped
½ teaspoon cayenne pepper
½ teaspoon ground cumin
1 teaspoon ground turmeric
½ teaspoon ground ginger
2 teaspoons paprika

2 tablespoons chopped flat-leaf
    (Italian) parsley
2 tablespoons chopped coriander
    (cilantro) leaves
2 tomatoes
500 g (1 lb 2 oz) orange sweet potatoes

Serves 4–6

Trim the steak of any fat and cut into 2.5 cm (1 in) pieces. Heat half the oil in a saucepan and brown the beef in batches over high heat, adding a little more oil as needed. Set aside in a dish.

Reduce the heat to low, add the onion and the remaining oil to the pan and gently cook for 10 minutes, or until the onion has softened. Add the cayenne pepper, cumin, turmeric, ginger and paprika, cook for a few seconds, then add 1 teaspoon salt and a good grinding of black pepper. Return the beef to the pan, along with the parsley, coriander and 250 ml (9 fl oz/1 cup) water. Cover and simmer over low heat for 1½ hours, or until the meat is almost tender.

Peel the tomatoes. To do this, score a cross in the base of each one using a knife. Put the tomatoes in a bowl of boiling water for 20 seconds, then plunge into a bowl of cold water to cool. Remove from the water and peel the skin away from the cross—the skin should slip off easily. Slice the tomatoes. Peel the sweet potatoes, cut them into 2 cm (¾ in) chunks and leave in cold water until required, as this will prevent them discolouring. Preheat the oven to 180°C (350°F/Gas 4).

Transfer the meat and its sauce to an ovenproof serving dish (the base of a tagine would be ideal). Drain the sweet potatoes and spread them on top of the beef. Top with the sliced tomatoes. Cover with foil (or the lid of the tagine) and bake for 40 minutes. Remove the foil, increase the oven temperature to 220°C (425°F/Gas 7) and raise the dish to the upper oven shelf. Cook until the tomatoes and sweet potatoes are flecked with brown and are tender. Serve from the dish.

preserves... The most famous of Morocco's preserves is *hamad m'rakad*, preserved lemons. The transformation of a whole lemon into a new ingredient, unique in taste and silken in texture, is achieved by preserving the lemons in a mixture of salt and lemon juice for up to six weeks (see page 251). In the *souks*, the preserved lemons are sold loose, packed neatly in piles.

Olives are picked when they are either green, half-ripe with a blush of red, uniformly red, or black to make cured olives of many hues and flavours. Some green olives are left whole or cracked to split the skin to hasten the pickling process. All of these are soaked in cold water for a number of days, the water changed daily. After the olives lose their initial bitterness, they are placed in a brine solution and left for two to three months. Black olives are also dry-salted without preliminary soaking. The olives are layered in baskets with salt, then covered and weighted, which helps to rid them of their bitter juices. Being so intense in flavour, these are the most popular olives. Cured olives are also prepared and sold with marinades of aromatics and herbs, or harissa.

Various vegetables are also preserved, pickled in a solution of brine and vinegar, similar to the vegetable pickles of the Middle East. These include sweet capsicums (peppers) and chillies, or diced mixed vegetables, such as turnips, carrots and cauliflowers.

Another preserve is *khlii*, Moroccan-style jerky. Beef or lamb strips are salted for 24 hours, then rubbed with a mixture of crushed garlic, ground cumin and coriander seeds. They are left for another 24 hours, then individually hung on a line to dry in the sun, covered in muslin (cheesecloth) for protection. It can take six days for all traces of moisture to be removed, with the

meat brought indoors each night. When completely dry, the meat is put in a large pot and covered with water and a mixture of olive oil and rendered beef and lamb fat, and cooked for two to three hours. The meat is removed and cooled, then transferred to pottery jars. The cooking liquid is boiled until only the fat remains, and this is poured over the meat. *Khlii* keeps for many months and is used in couscous, in tagines, with eggs, and in *rghayif*, filled savoury pancakes.

1.5 kg (3 lb 5 oz) ripe tomatoes
1 kg (2 lb 4 oz) lamb shoulder or
  leg steaks
2 tablespoons olive oil
2 onions, coarsely grated
2 garlic cloves, finely chopped
1 teaspoon ground ginger
¼ teaspoon freshly ground black pepper
1 cinnamon stick

¼ teaspoon ground saffron threads
3 tablespoons tomato paste
  (concentrated purée)
2 tablespoons honey
1½ teaspoons ground cinnamon
30 g (1 oz) butter
40 g (1½ oz/¼ cup) blanched almonds

Serves 4–6

Halve the tomatoes crossways and squeeze out the seeds. Coarsely grate the tomatoes into a bowl down to the skin, discarding the skin. Set aside.

Trim the lamb steaks and cut into 3 cm (1¼ in) pieces. Heat half the olive oil in a heavy-based saucepan over high heat and brown the lamb on each side, in batches. Set aside on a plate.

Reduce the heat to low, add the remaining olive oil and the onion and cook gently, stirring occasionally, for 10 minutes, or until the onion has softened. Stir in the garlic, ginger, black pepper and cinnamon stick and cook for 1 minute. Add the saffron, if using, and the tomato paste and cook for a further 1 minute. Return the lamb to the pan, along with the grated tomato, stir and season with salt and pepper. Cover and simmer gently for 1¼ hours. After this time, set the lid slightly ajar so that the pan is partly covered and continue to simmer for 15 minutes, stirring occasionally, then take the lid off and simmer for 25 minutes, or until the sauce has thickened. When it is very thick, almost jam-like in consistency with the oil beginning to separate, stir in the honey and ground cinnamon and simmer for 2 minutes.

Melt the butter in a small frying pan, add the almonds and cook over medium heat, stirring occasionally, until the almonds are golden. Tip immediately onto a plate to prevent them from burning.

Remove the cinnamon stick from the lamb, transfer to a serving dish and sprinkle with the almonds. Serve with crusty bread or couscous.

lamb tagine with sweet tomato jam

chicken k'dra
with chickpeas

60 g (2¼ oz) herbed smen (page 247)
   or butter
3 onions, thinly sliced
½ teaspoon ground ginger
½ teaspoon freshly ground black pepper
1.5 kg (3 lb 5 oz) chicken, quartered
¼ teaspoon ground saffron threads
1 cinnamon stick
2 x 420 g (15 oz) tins chickpeas
3 tablespoons finely chopped flat-leaf
   (Italian) parsley, plus extra, to serve
lemon wedges, to serve

Serves 4

Melt the smen in a large frying pan. Add a third of the onion and cook over medium heat for 5 minutes, or until softened. Add the ginger, black pepper and chicken pieces and cook without browning for 2–3 minutes, turning the chicken occasionally. Add the remaining onion, 310 ml (10¾ fl oz/1¼ cups) water, the saffron, cinnamon stick and 1 teaspoon salt. Bring to a slow boil, reduce the heat to low, then cover and simmer gently for 45 minutes.

Meanwhile, drain the chickpeas and place them in a large bowl with cold water to cover. Lift up handfuls of chickpeas and rub them between your hands to loosen the skins, dropping them back into the bowl. Run more water into the bowl, stir well and let the skins float to the top, then skim them off. Repeat until all the skins have been removed. Add the skinned chickpeas to the chicken, along with the parsley, stir gently, then cover and simmer for 15 minutes, or until the chicken is tender.

Tilt the saucepan and spoon off some of the fat from the surface and put it into a frying pan. Lift out the chicken pieces, allowing the sauce to drain back into the saucepan. Heat the fat in the frying pan and brown the chicken pieces quickly over high heat. Meanwhile, boil the sauce to reduce it a little.

Serve the chicken with the chickpeas and the sauce spooned over. Sprinkle with the extra parsley and serve with lemon wedges and crusty bread.

1.25 kg (2 lb 12 oz) lamb shoulder
 on the bone
1½ teaspoons ground cumin, plus extra
 to serve (optional)
1 teaspoon coarse salt, plus extra
 to serve (optional)
½ teaspoon freshly ground black pepper

pinch of ground saffron threads
6 garlic cloves, bruised
10–12 parsley stalks
1 tablespoon olive oil

Serves 4

Trim the excess fat from the whole shoulder of lamb if necessary. Wipe the meat with damp paper towels and then cut small incisions into the meat on each side.

Combine the cumin, salt, black pepper and saffron and rub the mixture into the lamb, pushing it into the incisions. Cover and leave for 30 minutes for the flavours to penetrate. Place the lamb, fat side up, on a piece of muslin (cheesecloth), top with half the garlic cloves and tie the muslin over the top.

Using a large saucepan onto which a steamer will fit, or the base of a couscoussier, fill it three-quarters full with water. If using a saucepan and steamer, check that the base of the steamer is at least 3 cm (1¼ in) above the surface of the water. Cover and bring to the boil. Line the base of the steamer with the parsley stalks and the remaining garlic cloves. Place the lamb on top, put folded strips of foil around the rim of the steamer and put the lid on firmly to contain the steam. Keeping the heat just high enough to maintain a boil, steam for 2–2½ hours—do not lift the lid for the first 1½ hours of cooking. The lamb should easily pull away from the bone when cooked. Lift it out of the steamer and remove the muslin.

Heat the oil in a large frying pan and quickly brown the lamb on each side for a more attractive presentation. This dish is traditionally served as part of a Moroccan meal, with the lamb taken from the bone with the fingers, accompanied with little dishes of coarse salt and ground cumin for extra seasoning. However, the lamb can be sliced and served with beetroot and cumin salad (page 51) and tiny boiled potatoes tossed with butter and chopped parsley.

steamed lamb
with cumin

chicken soup with couscous

1.5 kg (3 lb 5 oz) chicken
2 tablespoons olive oil
2 onions, finely chopped
½ teaspoon ground cumin
½ teaspoon paprika
½ teaspoon harissa (page 250), or to
    taste, or ¼ teaspoon cayenne pepper
2 tomatoes
1 tablespoon tomato paste
    (concentrated purée)
1 teaspoon sugar

1 cinnamon stick
100 g (3½ oz/½ cup) couscous
2 tablespoons finely chopped flat-leaf
    (Italian) parsley
1 tablespoon finely chopped coriander
    (cilantro) leaves
1 teaspoon dried mint
lemon wedges, to serve

Serves 4

Rinse the chicken under cold running water and drain. Joint the chicken into eight pieces by first removing both legs and cutting through the joint of the drumstick and the thigh. Cut down each side of the backbone and lift it out. Turn the chicken over and cut through the breastbone. Cut each breast in half, leaving the wing attached to the top half. Remove the skin and discard it.

Heat the olive oil in a large saucepan or stockpot, add the chicken and cook over high heat for 2–3 minutes, stirring often. Reduce the heat to medium, add the onion and cook for 5 minutes, or until the onion has softened. Stir in the cumin, paprika and harissa or cayenne pepper. Add 1 litre (35 fl oz/ 4 cups) water and bring to the boil.

Halve the tomatoes crossways and squeeze out the seeds. Coarsely grate the tomatoes over a plate down to the skin, discarding the skin. Add the grated tomato to the pan, along with the tomato paste, sugar, cinnamon stick, 1 teaspoon salt and some freshly ground black pepper. Bring to the boil, reduce the heat to low, then cover and simmer for 1 hour, or until the chicken is very tender.

Remove the chicken to a dish using a slotted spoon. When it is cool enough to handle, remove the bones and tear the chicken meat into strips. Return to the pan with an additional 500 ml (17 fl oz/2 cups) water and return to the boil. While it is boiling, gradually pour in the couscous, stirring constantly. Reduce the heat, then stir in the parsley, coriander and mint and simmer, uncovered, for 20 minutes. Adjust the seasoning and serve with lemon wedges to squeeze over, and crusty bread.

1 kg (2 lb 4 oz) beef chuck steak
3 tablespoons olive oil
1 onion, finely chopped
3 garlic cloves, finely chopped
½ teaspoon ground cumin
½ teaspoon ground turmeric
400 g (14 oz) tin chopped,
    peeled tomatoes
½ teaspoon sugar

1 cinnamon stick
2 tablespoons chopped flat-leaf (Italian)
    parsley
1 tablespoon chopped coriander (cilantro)
    leaves, plus extra leaves, to serve
500 g (1 lb 2 oz) small fresh okra

Serves 4–6

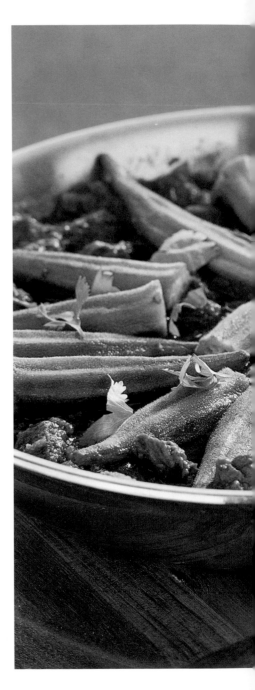

Trim the steak and cut it into 2.5 cm (1 in) pieces. Heat half the olive oil in a large saucepan over medium heat and brown the beef in batches, adding a little more oil as needed. Set aside in a dish.

Reduce the heat to low, add the onion and the remaining oil to the pan and cook gently for 10 minutes, or until softened. Add the garlic, cumin and turmeric, cook for a few seconds, then add the tomatoes, sugar, cinnamon stick, 1 teaspoon salt and a good grinding of black pepper. Return the beef to the pan, add the parsley, coriander and 250 ml (9 fl oz/1 cup) water. Cover the pan and simmer over low heat for 1½ hours, or until the meat is almost tender.

Meanwhile, trim the very ends of the okra stems—do not cut into the pods. Rinse the okra in a colander under cold running water. Check that there is sufficient liquid in the saucepan, add a little more water if necessary so that the meat is almost covered, and place the okra on top. Lightly sprinkle with a little salt, cover and simmer for a further 30 minutes. Do not stir during this stage of cooking.

Serve the meat with the okra arranged over the top. Scatter with the extra coriander leaves and serve with crusty bread.

beef tagine with okra and tomatoes

lamb tagine with peas and lemons

1 kg (2 lb 4 oz) lamb shoulder or
    leg, boned
2 tablespoons olive oil
1 onion, finely chopped
2 garlic cloves, finely chopped
1 teaspoon ground cumin
½ teaspoon ground ginger
½ teaspoon ground turmeric
3 tablespoons chopped coriander
    (cilantro) leaves
3 tablespoons chopped flat-leaf
    (Italian) parsley

1 teaspoon dried za'atar or 2 teaspoons
    chopped fresh lemon thyme
1½ preserved lemons (page 251)
235 g (8½ oz/1½ cups) shelled fresh or
    frozen green peas
2 teaspoons chopped mint
½ teaspoon sugar

Serves 4–6

Trim the lamb and cut into 3 cm (1¼ in) pieces. Heat the olive oil in a large saucepan over high heat and brown the lamb in batches, removing to a dish when cooked. Add more oil if required.

Reduce the heat to low, add the onion and cook for 5 minutes until softened. Add the garlic, cumin, ginger and turmeric and cook for a few seconds. Add 375 ml (13 fl oz/1½ cups) water and stir well to lift the browned juices off the base of the pan, then return the lamb to pan with a little salt and a good grinding of black pepper. Add the coriander, parsley and za'atar or thyme, then cover and simmer over low heat for 1½ hours, or until the lamb is tender.

Separate the preserved lemons into quarters and rinse well under cold running water, removing and discarding the pulp and membranes. Cut the rind into strips and add to the lamb, along with the peas, mint and sugar. Return to a simmer, cover and simmer for a further 10 minutes, or until the peas are cooked. Serve hot.

4 zucchini (courgettes)
2 small capsicums (peppers)
6 tomatoes

LAMB STUFFING
2 tablespoons olive oil
1 onion, finely chopped
2 garlic cloves, finely chopped
½ teaspoon ground ginger
½ teaspoon ground cinnamon
¼ teaspoon freshly ground black pepper
500 g (1 lb 2 oz) minced (ground) lamb
  or beef
2 tablespoons chopped flat-leaf
  (Italian) parsley
1 tablespoon chopped coriander
  (cilantro) leaves

2 teaspoons chopped mint
55 g (2 oz/¼ cup) short-grain rice

TOMATO SAUCE
1 tablespoon olive oil
1 onion, coarsely grated
1 garlic clove, finely chopped
½ teaspoon paprika
¼ teaspoon ground cumin
1 large tomato, peeled, seeded
  (pages 48–9) and chopped
2 tablespoons tomato paste
  (concentrated purée)
1 teaspoon sugar
1 tablespoon lemon juice

Serves 4

Halve the zucchini lengthways. Scoop out the centres, leaving a 1 cm (½ in) border. Halve the capsicums lengthways; remove the seeds and membranes. Slice the tops from four tomatoes (reserve the tops), scoop out the centres and rub the pulp through a sieve into a bowl. Remove the skin from the remaining tomatoes (pages 48–9), slice them thinly and set aside.

To make the stuffing, put the oil and onion in a saucepan over medium heat and cook for 5 minutes. Stir in the garlic, ginger, cinnamon, pepper and meat. Add 250 ml (9 fl oz/1 cup) water, parsley, coriander, mint and 1 teaspoon salt. Bring to the boil, then cover and simmer over low heat for 20 minutes. Stir in the rice, cover, and cook for 10 minutes, or until most of the liquid is absorbed.

To make the sauce, add all the sauce ingredients and 125 ml (4 fl oz/½ cup) water to the tomato pulp. Season. Preheat the oven to 180°C (350°F/Gas 4).

Loosely fill the vegetables with the stuffing. Fill four zucchini halves and top with an unfilled half, securing with wooden cocktail picks. Fill the capsicums and arrange tomato slices over the top; fill the tomatoes and replace the tops. Arrange in an ovenproof dish. Pour in the sauce, cover with foil and bake for 50 minutes, then remove the foil, baste with sauce and cook for 10 minutes,

vegetables with lamb stuffing

meatball tagine with herbs and lemon

½ **onion, roughly chopped**
2 **tablespoons roughly chopped flat-leaf**
  (Italian) parsley
2 **slices white bread, crusts removed**
1 **egg**
500 g (1 lb 2 oz) **minced (ground) lamb**
  or beef
½ **teaspoon ground cumin**
½ **teaspoon paprika**
½ **teaspoon freshly ground black pepper**

HERB AND LEMON SAUCE
1 **tablespoon butter or oil**
½ **onion, finely chopped**
½ **teaspoon paprika**

½ **teaspoon ground turmeric**
¼ **teaspoon ground cumin**
1 **red chilli, seeded and sliced, or**
  ¼ **teaspoon cayenne pepper**
375 ml (13 fl oz/1½ cups) **chicken stock**
  or water
2 **tablespoons chopped coriander**
  (cilantro) leaves
2 **tablespoons chopped flat-leaf**
  (Italian) parsley
2 **tablespoons lemon juice**
½ **preserved lemon (page 251) (optional)**

Serves 4

Put the onion and parsley in the food processor bowl and process until finely chopped. Tear the bread into pieces, add to the bowl with the egg and process briefly. Add the meat, cumin, paprika, black pepper and 1 teaspoon salt and process to a thick paste, scraping down the side of the bowl occasionally. Alternatively, grate the onion, chop the parsley, crumb the bread and add to the mince in a bowl with the egg, spices and seasoning. Knead until paste-like in consistency.

With moistened hands, shape the mixture into walnut-sized balls and place them on a tray. Cover and refrigerate until required.

To make the herb and lemon sauce, heat the butter or oil in a saucepan and add the onion. Cook over low heat until softened and golden, then add the paprika, turmeric, cumin and chilli or cayenne pepper and cook, stirring, for 1 minute. Add the stock and coriander and bring to the boil.

Add the meatballs, shaking the pan so that they settle into the sauce. Cover and simmer for 45 minutes. Add most of the parsley and the lemon juice and season if necessary. Return to the boil and simmer for 2 minutes. If using preserved lemon, rinse well under running water, remove and discard the pulp and membrane and cut the rind into strips. Add to the meatballs. Transfer to a tagine or bowl, scatter with the remaining parsley and serve with crusty bread.

3 teaspoons active dried yeast
375 ml (13 fl oz/1½ cups) lukewarm
  water
410 g (14½ oz/3⅓ cups) strong flour
  or plain (all-purpose) flour, preferably
  unbleached
200 g (7 oz/1⅓ cups) wholemeal
  (whole wheat) flour

125 ml (4 fl oz/½ cup) lukewarm milk
2 tablespoons polenta
1 tablespoon whole aniseed, toasted
  sesame seeds, black sesame seeds
  or coarse salt for topping breads

Makes 3 loaves

Dissolve the yeast in 125 ml (4 fl oz/½ cup) of the lukewarm water. Sift the flours and 1½ teaspoons salt into a large mixing bowl and make a well in the centre. Pour the yeast mixture into the well, then add the remaining 250 ml (9 fl oz/1 cup) water and the milk. Stir sufficient flour into the liquid to form a thin batter, cover the bowl with a cloth and set aside for 15 minutes until bubbles form.

Gradually stir in the remaining flour, then mix with your hands to form a soft dough, adding a little extra water if necessary. Turn out onto a lightly floured work surface and knead for 10 minutes, or until smooth and elastic and the dough springs back when an impression is made with a finger. Only knead in extra plain flour if the dough remains sticky after a few minutes of kneading.

As the dough requires only one rising, divide into three even-sized pieces. Shape each piece into a ball and roll out on a lightly floured work surface to rounds 23 cm (9 in) in diameter or 26 cm (10½ in) for flatter breads.

Sift the polenta onto baking trays. Lift the rounds onto the trays, reshaping if necessary. Brush the tops lightly with water and, if desired, sprinkle with any one of the toppings, pressing it in lightly. Cover the loaves with tea towels (dish towels) and leave in a warm, draught-free place for 1 hour to rise. The bread has risen sufficiently when a depression remains in the dough after it is pressed lightly with a fingertip.

While the loaves are rising, preheat the oven to 220°C (425°F/Gas 7). Just before baking, prick the breads in several places with a fork. Put the breads in the hot oven and bake for 12–15 minutes, or until the bread is golden and sounds hollow when the base is tapped. Cool on a wire rack. Cut in wedges to serve. Use on the day of baking. Any leftover loaves may be frozen.

moroccan bread

filled
savoury pancakes

2 teaspoons active dried yeast
250 ml (9 fl oz/1 cup) lukewarm water
1 teaspoon sugar
300 g (10½ oz/2⅓ cups) plain
   (all-purpose) flour
olive oil, for coating
oil, for frying
lemon wedges, to serve

SPICED KEFTA
80 g (2¾ oz) smen (page 247) or ghee
250 g (9 oz) finely minced (ground) beef
2 tablespoons grated onion
4 garlic cloves, finely chopped
2 teaspoons ground cumin
2 teaspoons ground coriander

Makes 12

Dissolve the yeast in 125 ml (4 fl oz/½ cup) of the lukewarm water and stir in the sugar. Sift the flour and ½ teaspoon salt in a shallow bowl and make a well in the centre. Pour the yeast mixture into the well, then add the remaining water. Stir sufficient flour into the liquid to form a thin batter, cover the bowl with a cloth and leave for 15 minutes until bubbles form. Gradually stir in the remaining flour, then mix with your hands until a sticky dough is formed. If too stiff, add a little more water. Knead for 10 minutes in the bowl until smooth and elastic. Pour a little olive oil down the side of the bowl, turn the ball of dough to coat in the oil, then cover and leave in a warm place for 30 minutes.

To make the spiced kefta, heat the smen or ghee in a frying pan, add the beef and stir over high heat until browned. Reduce the heat to low, add the onion, garlic, cumin, coriander and season with salt and pepper. Cook, stirring, for 2 minutes, then add 500 ml (17 fl oz/2 cups) water. Cover and simmer for 30–45 minutes until the water evaporates and the fat separates. Tip into a food processor and process to a paste; alternatively, pound to a paste in a mortar. Set aside to cool.

Using oiled hands, punch down the dough and divide into 12 balls. Oil the work surface and the rolling pin and roll out and stretch a dough ball into an 18 cm (7 in) circle. Spread thinly with a tablespoon of kefta paste. Fold the sides in so that they overlap, then fold in the top and bottom to overlap in the centre. Roll out and shape into a 9 x 13 cm (3½ x 5 in) rectangle. Place on an oiled tray and repeat with the remaining ingredients.

In a frying pan, add the oil to a depth of 1 cm (½ in). Place over high heat and, when almost smoking, reduce the heat to medium and add two pancakes. Cook for about 1 minute per side, or until browned and crisp and cooked through. Drain on paper towels and serve hot with lemon wedges.

4 teaspoons active dried yeast
500 ml (17 fl oz/2 cups) lukewarm water
210 g (7½ oz/1⅓ cups) plain (all-purpose)
   flour
210 g (7½ oz/1⅓ cups) very fine semolina
2 eggs

125 ml (4 fl oz/½ cup) lukewarm milk
oil, for coating
unsalted butter, to serve
warm honey, to serve

Makes 16

Dissolve the yeast in 125 ml (4 fl oz/½ cup) of the lukewarm water and mix in 3 teaspoons of the flour. Cover with a cloth and leave in a warm place for 15 minutes until frothy.

Sift the remaining flour, semolina and salt into a mixing bowl and make a well in the centre. Beat the eggs lightly with the lukewarm milk and pour into the flour mixture, then add the yeast mixture and remaining water. Starting with the flour surrounding the well and working outwards, bring the flour into the liquid, then beat well with a balloon whisk for 5–7 minutes until smooth. The batter should have the consistency of thick cream. Cover the bowl with a folded tea towel (dish towel) and leave in a warm place for 1 hour, or until doubled in bulk and bubbles form.

Fill a saucepan one-third full with water, bring to a simmer, then place a large heatproof plate over the top. Put a tea towel, folded in quarters, on the plate.

Heat a heavy cast-iron frying pan or crepe pan over high heat. Reduce the heat to medium and rub the pan with a wad of paper towels dipped in oil. Pour in a small ladleful (about 3 tablespoons) of batter and, using the bottom of the ladle, quickly shape into a round about 15 cm (6 in) in diameter. Work quickly and try to make the top as even as possible. Cook until the top of the pancake looks dry and is peppered with little holes from the bubbles. While it is not traditional, you can turn it over and briefly brown the bubbly side.

Remove the pancake to the folds of the tea towel, bubbly side up, and cover to keep warm. Overlap the pancakes rather than stack them. Repeat with the remaining batter, oiling the pan with the wad of paper towels between each pancake. Serve hot with butter and warm honey.

semolina pancakes

rice pudding with raisins

110 g (3¾ oz/½ cup) short-grain rice
1.125 litres (39 fl oz/4½ cups) milk
55 g (2 oz/¼ cup) sugar
55 g (2 oz/½ cup) ground almonds
2 tablespoons cornflour (cornstarch)
¼ teaspoon almond extract
2 tablespoons orange flower water
2 tablespoons raisins
2 tablespoons honey

Serves 8

Put the rice in a large heavy-based saucepan with 250 ml (9 fl oz/1 cup) water and a pinch of salt. Place over medium heat and cook for 5 minutes, stirring occasionally, until the water has been absorbed.

Set aside 125 ml (4 fl oz/½ cup) of the milk. Stir 250 ml (9 fl oz/1 cup) of the remaining milk into the rice, bring to a simmer, and when the rice has absorbed the milk, add another 250 ml (9 fl oz/1 cup) milk. Continue to cook the rice until all the milk has been added, ensuring each addition of milk is absorbed before adding the next. (Adding the milk gradually helps prevent the milk from boiling over.) The rice should be very soft in 30 minutes, with the final addition of milk barely absorbed.

Mix the sugar with the ground almonds to break up any lumps in the almonds. Stir into the rice mixture and simmer gently for 2–3 minutes. Mix the cornflour with the reserved milk and stir into the rice. When thickened, boil gently for 2 minutes. Remove the pan from the heat and stir in the almond extract and 1½ tablespoons of the orange flower water. Stir the pudding occasionally to cool it a little.

Meanwhile, steep the raisins in the remaining 2 teaspoons of orange flower water for 15 minutes. Pour the pudding into a serving bowl and when a slight skin forms on the top, sprinkle with the soaked raisins and drizzle with honey. Cool completely before serving in individual bowls.

500 ml (17 fl oz/2 cups) milk
3 tablespoons caster (superfine) sugar
2 tablespoons cornflour (cornstarch)
1 tablespoon ground rice
70 g (2½ oz/⅔ cup) ground almonds
1 teaspoon rosewater
2 tablespoons slivered (or flaked)
   almonds, toasted
1 teaspoon caster (superfine) sugar, extra
½ teaspoon ground cinnamon

Serves 4

Put the milk and sugar in a heavy-based saucepan and heat over medium heat until the sugar has dissolved. Bring to the boil.

In a large bowl, combine the cornflour and ground rice with 3 tablespoons water and mix to a smooth paste. Pour in the boiling milk, stirring constantly with a balloon whisk, then return to the saucepan. Stir over medium heat until thickened and bubbling, then add the ground almonds and simmer over low heat for 5 minutes, stirring occasionally. Add the rosewater and remove from the heat. Stir occasionally to cool a little, then spoon into serving bowls. Refrigerate for 1 hour.

Mix the toasted almonds with the extra sugar and the cinnamon and sprinkle over the top before serving.

mulhalabia

a little taste of...

The legendary Moroccan hospitality is more than adequately demonstrated at a *diffa*, or banquet. Betrothals, weddings, births and religious festivals are occasions to celebrate with an abundance of food. Especially lavish *diffas* are given when a Moroccan returns from a pilgrimage to Mecca. Seated around low, round tables, on divans luxurious with multicoloured cushions, guests feast on *zeilook*, eggplant (aubergine) salad; *bessara*, broad (fava) bean dip; *mohkt*, a salad of lamb's brains — all scooped up with morsels of bread; as well as crisp, golden briouats with savoury fillings; and an abundance of salads to be picked at delicately. *Bisteeya*, a savoury pigeon or chicken pie, is served on its own in all its glory, as it is considered one of the high points of Moroccan cuisine. Tagines of meat, poultry and fish follow, including at least one that is sweet with fruit and honey. And to ensure that appetites are satisfied, couscous is served. Grape, pomegranate or other juices may be offered during the meal. Platters of fresh fruit complete the feast, followed by sweet pastries and mint tea.

...banquet food

briouats
with seafood

FISH OR PRAWN FILLING
250 g (9 oz) boneless white fish fillets,
    or 200 g (7 oz) cooked, shelled prawns
    (shrimp)
2 tablespoons finely chopped flat-leaf
    (Italian) parsley
1 tablespoon finely chopped spring onion
    (scallion)
1 garlic clove, crushed
½ teaspoon paprika
¼ teaspoon ground cumin
pinch of cayenne pepper

1 tablespoon lemon juice
1 tablespoon olive oil

6 sheets filo pastry
1 egg white, lightly beaten
oil, for deep-frying
3 tablespoons caster (superfine) sugar,
    to serve
⅛ teaspoon cayenne pepper, to serve
1 teaspoon ground cinnamon, to serve

Makes 24

To make the fish or prawn filling, first poach the fish gently in lightly salted water, to cover, until the flesh flakes—about 4–5 minutes. Remove from the poaching liquid to a plate and cover closely with plastic wrap so that the surface does not dry as it cools. When cool, flake the fish and put it in a bowl. If using cooked prawns, cut them into small pieces. Put the fish or the prawns in a bowl, add the parsley, spring onion, garlic, paprika, cumin, cayenne pepper, lemon juice and olive oil and toss well to mix.

Stack the filo sheets on a cutting board, and with a ruler and sharp knife, measure and cut across the width of the pastry to give strips 12 cm (4½ in) wide and 28–30 cm (11¼–12 in) long. Stack the cut filo in the folds of a damp tea towel (dish towel) or cover with plastic wrap to prevent it from drying out.

Take a filo strip and, with the narrow end towards you, fold it in half across its width to make a strip 6 cm (2½ in) wide. Place a generous teaspoon of filling 2 cm (¾ in) in from the base of the strip, fold the end diagonally across the filling so that the base lines up with the side of the strip, forming a triangle. Fold straight up once, then fold diagonally to the opposite side. Continue folding until near the end of the strip, then brush the filo lightly with egg white and complete the fold. Place on a cloth-covered tray, seam side down. Cover with a tea towel until ready to fry, and cook within 10 minutes.

Heat the oil to 180°C (350°F), or until a cube of bread dropped into the oil browns in 15 seconds. Add four briouats at a time and fry until golden, turning to brown evenly. Remove with a slotted spoon; drain on paper towels.

3 sweet oranges
500 g (1 lb 2 oz) carrots
2 tablespoons lemon juice
1 teaspoon ground cinnamon,
  plus extra, to serve
1 tablespoon caster (superfine) sugar
1 tablespoon orange flower water
small mint leaves, to serve

Serves 6

Cut off the tops and bases of the oranges. Cut the peel off using a sharp knife, removing all traces of pith and cutting through the outer membranes to expose the flesh. Holding the orange over a bowl to catch the juice, segment the oranges by cutting between the membranes. Remove the seeds and place the segments in the bowl. Squeeze the remains of the orange to extract all the juice. Pour the juice into another bowl.

Peel and julienne the carrots using a sharp knife. Put the carrots in the bowl with the orange juice. Add the lemon juice, cinnamon, sugar, orange flower water and a small pinch of salt. Stir well to combine. Cover the carrot mixture and oranges and refrigerate until required.

Just before serving, drain off the accumulated juice from the oranges and arrange the segments around the edge of a serving dish. Pile the shredded carrots in the centre and top with the mint leaves. Dust the oranges lightly with a little of the extra cinnamon.

orange and carrot salad

baked fish
with tomatoes

1 kg (2 lb 4 oz) whole white-fleshed fish,
  such as snapper or bream, scaled
  and cleaned
3 garlic cloves, crushed
2 teaspoons harissa (page 250),
  or to taste
2 tablespoons olive oil
1 lemon, thinly sliced
1 onion, thinly sliced
2 large firm, ripe tomatoes, sliced
4 thyme sprigs

Serves 4

Preheat the oven to 200°C (400°F/Gas 6). Lightly grease a large baking dish. Make three diagonal cuts on each side of the fish through the thickest part of the flesh to ensure even cooking.

Combine the garlic, harissa and olive oil in a small dish. Put 2 teaspoons of the harissa mixture in the fish cavity and spread the remainder over both sides of the fish, rubbing it into the slits. Place two lemon slices in the cavity of the fish.

Arrange the onion slices in a layer on the baking dish. Top with the tomato slices, thyme and remaining lemon slices. Place the fish on top and bake, uncovered, for about 25–30 minutes, or until the flesh is opaque.

Transfer the onion and tomato to a serving dish. Place the fish on top and season with salt.

fasts and feasts... Ramadan is the ninth month of the Muslim year, commemorating Mohammed's first revelations that make up the Koran. For 30 days, Moroccans fast from dawn to dusk — no food or drink, no smoking and no other earthly pleasures. In the cities, a cannon is fired at sunset and the *ftur*, the first meal, begins. *Harira*, chickpea and lamb soup, is the Moroccan's break fast tradition, with bread, dates, milk and *shebbakia*, fried rosettes of yeast dough, honey-dipped and sprinkled with sesame seeds. Another meal is taken later at night, and the morning meal is eaten before dawn — usually leftovers, with bread, hard-boiled eggs with cumin, dates and sweet fried doughs to fortify the body for the denials of the coming day.

Aid el kebir is the festival of the sacrifice of the lamb, a five-day festival commemorating Abraham's sacrifice, held 50 days after Ramadan. Each household buys at least one lamb. On the first day of the festival, a slaughterer is hired to kill the lamb according to Islamic law. Grilled liver kebabs and a tripe tagine are the first dishes prepared and, over the ensuing days, all the lamb is consumed, including the trotters. One particular dish, *mrouzia*, is cooked on the last day using the leftover lamb. It contains large amounts of raisins and honey, and the high sugar content preserves it for a month or more.

Berber tribes have their *moussems* — festivals and pilgrimages — where feasting is just part of the festivities. They travel to the chosen site and set up a tent city for the duration of the festival. The highlight is *mechoui*, whole lamb rubbed with garlic and spices and spit-roasted over a charcoal fire, basted with smen until meltingly tender.

For any meal, there are rules to follow, with slight changes according to the occasion. Firstly, hands must be washed. At a formal gathering a servant or young family member circulates with a jug of warm, rose-scented water, a basin and towel. Dishes are served on a central platter, in a tagine or in shallow bowls placed in the middle of the table. Before eating begins, the host gives the blessing 'Bismillah' — 'in the name of Allah'. Food is picked from the communal dish with the thumb and first two fingers of the right hand and popped into the mouth, with each diner taking food from the section of the dish nearest him. Fingers are wiped on bread if necessary — never licked until the meal is completed — and the bread is dipped in the sauce and eaten. Hands are washed again at the end of the meal before retiring to the reception room for mint tea and pastries.

2 x 450 g (1 lb) eggplants (aubergines)
3 tomatoes
olive oil, for frying
2 garlic cloves, finely chopped
1 teaspoon paprika
½ teaspoon ground cumin
¼ teaspoon cayenne pepper, or to taste

2 tablespoons finely chopped coriander
   (cilantro) leaves
2½ tablespoons lemon juice
½ preserved lemon (page 251) (optional)
   or fresh lemon slices, to serve

Serves 6–8

Using a vegetable peeler, remove 1 cm (½ in) wide strips of skin along the length of each eggplant. Cut the eggplants into 1 cm (½ in) slices, sprinkle with salt and layer the slices in a colander. Leave for 20–30 minutes, then rinse under cold running water. Drain, squeeze the slices gently, then pat them dry with paper towels.

Peel the tomatoes by first scoring a cross in the base of each one using a knife. Put in a bowl of boiling water for 20 seconds, then plunge into a bowl of cold water to cool. Remove from the water and peel the skin away from the cross—it should slip off easily. Cut the tomatoes in half crossways and squeeze out the seeds. Chop the tomatoes and set aside.

Heat the olive oil in a frying pan to a depth of 5 mm (¼ in). Fry the eggplant slices in batches until browned on each side and set aside on a plate. Add more oil to the pan as needed.

Using the oil left in the pan, cook the garlic over low heat for a few seconds. Add the tomatoes, paprika, cumin and cayenne pepper and increase the heat to medium. Add the eggplant slices and cook, mashing the eggplant and tomato gently with a fork. Continue to cook until most of the liquid has evaporated. When the oil separates, drain off some if it seems excessive; however, some oil should be left in as it adds to the flavour of the dish. Add the coriander and lemon juice and season with freshly ground black pepper and a little salt if necessary. Transfer to a serving bowl.

If using preserved lemon, rinse under cold running water and remove the pulp and membranes. Chop the rind into small pieces and scatter over the eggplant or, alternatively, garnish with slices of fresh lemon. Serve warm or at room temperature with bread.

warm
eggplant salad

lemon, parsley and onion salad

6 lemons
1 small red onion
1 teaspoon caster (superfine) sugar
2 large handfuls flat-leaf (Italian) parsley,
   chopped

Serves 6–8

Peel the lemons with a sharp knife, making sure that all the pith and fine membranes are removed, to expose the flesh. Cut the lemons into 1 cm (½ in) thick slices and remove the seeds. Dice the lemon slices and put them in a bowl.

Halve the onion, then slice it thinly. Add to the lemons, along with the sugar, parsley and 1 teaspoon salt. Toss and set aside for 10 minutes.

Just before serving, lightly sprinkle with freshly ground black pepper. Serve with fish or as a refreshing, tart contrast to tagines that contain fruit.

CHEESE FILLING
250 g (9 oz) fresh goat's cheese
3 tablespoons finely chopped flat-leaf
    (Italian) parsley
2 teaspoons finely chopped mint
½ teaspoon paprika
¼ teaspoon freshly ground black pepper
1 egg, lightly beaten

24 won ton wrappers
1 egg white, lightly beaten
oil, for deep-frying

Makes 24

To make the cheese filling, mix the cheese with the parsley, mint, paprika
and black pepper. Check for salt and add if necessary. Stir in the beaten
egg gradually, adding just enough to retain a fairly stiff mixture—if too loose,
the rolls will be difficult to shape.

Put a stack of won ton wrappers in the folds of a tea towel (dish towel) to
prevent them drying out, or cover them with plastic wrap. Place a wrapper
on the work surface with one corner of the square towards you and brush
around the edge with the egg white. Put 2 teaspoons of cheese filling across
the corner, just meeting the sides. Roll once, turn each side of the wrapper
over the filling and roll to the end. Place on a cloth-covered tray, seam side
down. Continue in this manner with the remaining ingredients.

Heat the oil to 180°C (350°F), or until a cube of bread dropped into the hot
oil browns in 15 seconds. Add four briouats at a time and fry until golden,
turning to brown evenly. Remove with a slotted spoon and drain on paper
towels. Serve hot.

briouats with goat's cheese

mezghaldi of onions with eggplant

4 onions
100 ml (3½ fl oz) olive oil
½ teaspoon ground saffron threads
1 teaspoon ground ginger
1 teaspoon ground cinnamon
½ teaspoon ground allspice
1½ tablespoons honey
600 g (1 lb 5 oz) long thin eggplants
  (aubergines)

Serves 4

Halve the onions lengthways and cut them into slender wedges. Put them in a frying pan, cover with cold water and bring to the boil. Cover and simmer for 5 minutes. Drain the onion in a colander.

Add 2 tablespoons of the olive oil to the pan and, over low heat, stir in the ground saffron, ginger, cinnamon and allspice. Cook for 1 minute, then increase the heat to medium and return the onion to the pan. Add the honey and 375 ml (13 fl oz/1½ cups) water and season with salt and freshly ground black pepper. Stir well, reduce the heat to low, cover and simmer for 40 minutes, then uncover and simmer for 10 minutes, or until most of the liquid has evaporated.

Wash and dry the eggplants. Leaving the green stalks on for effect, halve them lengthways. Using the remaining oil, brush all the eggplant halves on each side. Cook the eggplants in a heated chargrill pan or on a barbecue grill for 3–4 minutes each side until they are tender, adjusting the heat so they do not burn.

Arrange the eggplants, cut side up, on a platter or on individual plates and season lightly with salt. Top with the onion and pour over any juices from the pan. Serve hot or warm with crusty bread, or as an accompaniment to chicken or chargrilled meats.

6 sweet oranges
2 teaspoons orange flower water
8 fresh dates, pitted and thinly
   sliced lengthways
90 g (3¼ oz/¾ cup) slivered almonds,
   lightly toasted
small mint leaves, to serve

Serves 4–6

Cut off the tops and bases of the oranges. Cut the peel off with a sharp knife, removing all traces of pith and cutting through the outer membranes to expose the flesh. Holding the orange over a bowl to catch any juice, segment the oranges by cutting between the visible membranes. Remove the seeds and place the segments in the bowl. Squeeze the remains of the oranges over the bowl to extract all the juice.

Add the orange flower water and stir gently to combine. Cover with plastic wrap and refrigerate until chilled.

Place the segments and the juice in a large flat dish and scatter the dates and almonds over the top. Sprinkle the mint leaves over the orange segments. Serve chilled.

orange and date salad

harira

500 g (1 lb 2 oz) lamb shoulder steaks
2 tablespoons olive oil
2 small onions, chopped
2 large garlic cloves, crushed
1½ teaspoons ground cumin
2 teaspoons paprika
1 bay leaf
2 tablespoons tomato paste
   (concentrated purée)
1 litre (35 fl oz/4 cups) beef stock

3 x 300 g (10½ oz) tins chickpeas
2 x 400 g (14 oz) tins chopped tomatoes
3 tablespoons finely chopped coriander
   (cilantro) leaves
3 tablespoons finely chopped flat-leaf
   (Italian) parsley
coriander (cilantro) leaves, extra, to serve
flat bread, to serve

Serves 4

Trim the lamb steaks of excess fat and sinew. Cut the lamb into small chunks.

Heat the olive oil in a large heavy-based saucepan or stockpot, add the onion and garlic and cook over low heat for 5 minutes, or until the onion is soft. Add the meat, increase the heat to medium and stir until the meat changes colour.

Add the cumin, paprika and bay leaf to the pan and cook until fragrant. Add the tomato paste and cook for about 2 minutes, stirring constantly. Add the beef stock to the pan, stir well and bring to the boil.

Drain the chickpeas, rinse them and add to the pan, along with the tomatoes and chopped coriander and parsley. Stir, then bring to the boil. Reduce the heat and simmer for 2 hours, or until the meat is tender. Stir occasionally. Season, to taste. Garnish with the extra coriander and serve with bread.

150 g (5½ oz) smen (page 247) or butter
1.5 kg (3 lb 5 oz) chicken, quartered, or
   3 x 500 g (1 lb 2 oz) squab (pigeon),
   halved
2 large red onions, finely chopped
3 garlic cloves, crushed
1 cinnamon stick
1 teaspoon ground ginger
1½ teaspoons ground cumin
¼ teaspoon cayenne pepper
½ teaspoon ground turmeric
large pinch of saffron threads, soaked in
   2 tablespoons warm water
500 ml (17 fl oz/2 cups) chicken stock
1 tablespoon lemon juice

2 large handfuls flat-leaf (Italian) parsley,
   chopped
2 large handfuls coriander (cilantro)
   leaves, chopped
5 eggs, lightly beaten
100 g (3½ oz/⅔ cup) almonds, toasted
   and finely chopped
3 tablespoons icing (confectioners') sugar,
   plus extra, to serve
1 teaspoon ground cinnamon,
   plus extra, to serve
12 sheets filo pastry
100 g (3½ oz) smen, extra, melted

Serves 6–8

Preheat the oven to 160°C (315°F/Gas 2–3). Melt the smen in a flameproof casserole dish over medium heat and brown the chicken or squab well. Set aside. Add the onion and cook until golden. Stir in the garlic and spices, then stir in the saffron, its soaking liquid, and the stock. Add the chicken and turn to coat. Cover and put in the oven for 1 hour, turning occasionally, or until cooked. Add a little extra water if needed. Remove the chicken, reserving the sauce. Discard the cinnamon stick. Remove the meat from the bones and cut into small pieces. Increase the oven temperature to 180°C (350°F/Gas 4).

Add the lemon juice and herbs to the sauce and reduce over high heat for 10 minutes until thick. Reduce the heat to very low, gradually stir in the eggs, stirring until scrambled, then remove from the heat. Add the meat and season.

Mix the almonds with the icing sugar and cinnamon. Brush a 1.5 litre (52 fl oz/6 cup) round deep pie or baking dish with smen. Put a filo sheet over the dish so the edges overhang; brush with smen. Repeat with seven more sheets, brushing with smen and working in a gradual clockwise motion, slightly overlapping the sheets to give a pinwheel effect. Fill with the chicken mixture and smooth over. Fold four of the filo flaps back over, brush with smen and sprinkle with the sugar mixture. Fold the remaining four sheets over; tuck the edges down into the dish. Brush four filo sheets with smen, cut into 15 cm (6 in) squares and scrunch into 'flowers' to cover the pie. Bake for 1 hour, or until golden. Serve sprinkled with the combined extra icing sugar and cinnamon.

bisteeya

lamb with eggs and almonds

1.25 kg (2 lb 12 oz) lamb shoulder steaks
3 tablespoons olive oil
2 onions, coarsely grated
3 garlic cloves, finely chopped
2 teaspoons ground ginger
¼ teaspoon ground saffron threads
1 large handful coriander (cilantro) leaves,
    chopped
40 g (1½ oz) butter
150 g (5½ oz/1 cup) blanched almonds
6 hard-boiled eggs
coriander (cilantro) leaves, extra, to serve

Serves 6

Trim the excess fat from the chops. Heat half the olive oil in a large saucepan over high heat and brown the lamb on each side in batches, removing to a dish when cooked. Add a little more oil as required.

Reduce the heat to low, add the remaining oil and the onion and cook for 5 minutes, or until the onion has softened. Add the garlic and ginger and cook for a few seconds. Pour in 375 ml (13 fl oz/1½ cups) water and stir to lift the browned juices off the base of the pan. Return the lamb to the pan, along with the saffron, 1 teaspoon salt and a good grinding of black pepper. Cover and simmer over low heat for 1¼ hours, then stir in the coriander and cook for a further 15 minutes, or until the lamb is tender.

Meanwhile, melt the butter in a frying pan over medium heat, add the almonds and fry them, tossing frequently, until golden. Remove immediately to a bowl to prevent them overbrowning. Shell and halve the boiled eggs.

Arrange the lamb on a serving dish, spoon the sauce over and sprinkle with the almonds (warm the almonds a little first if the butter has congealed). Arrange the eggs on top and scatter with a few coriander leaves.

tagines and couscoussiers... Two cooking utensils that define Moroccan cooking are the tagine and the couscoussier, both Berber in origin. The *tagine slaoui* is a shallow glazed earthenware cooking pot that sits on a *majmar*, a charcoal brazier of unglazed earthenware. It has a conical lid with the top fashioned into a knob so that it can be removed easily with one hand when the simmering food has to be checked. Steam condenses inside the lid, falling back into the simmering food. The food cooked in these earthenware pots is called a tagine, or Moroccan stew.

The *tagine slaoui* can be small enough to cook a single serve or large enough to cook for a dozen or more. Many cooks these days use a saucepan for cooking the stew, then transfer it to the tagine for serving. The shallow design of the dish allows easy access to the food with the fingers when eating.

The couscoussier is made of tinned copper or aluminium and resembles a tall, slightly bulbous boiler with a lid. The boiler section is called the *gdra*. A steamer, the *kskas*, fits into it. The stew is cooked in the lower boiler section, and the soaked couscous grains are placed in the steamer on top and left uncovered as the couscous steams. If you don't have one, any large saucepan with a steamer or colander placed on top can be used instead.

Another cooking pot of interest is the *tangia*, which, like the tagine, is also the name given to the food that is cooked in it. This is made of pottery and is shaped like a bulbous Grecian urn, tapering to a narrow neck, and has two handles. Little preparation is required: meat pieces, with various other ingredients, are put into the *tangia*, a piece of parchment is tied on top and it is then taken to the *hamman*, steam bath. The dish is placed amongst the embers in the furnace room and left for 8 hours or more to cook very slowly. Tangia was traditionally considered a bachelor's dish — its ease of preparation and cooking made it popular with unmarried men, soldiers and travellers who all had to fend for themselves.

1.6 kg (3 lb 8 oz) chicken
3 tablespoons smen (page 247) or ghee
1 onion, finely chopped
½ teaspoon ground turmeric
½ teaspoon ground cumin
8 baby onions, trimmed
¼ teaspoon ground saffron threads
1 cinnamon stick
4 coriander (cilantro) sprigs and 4 flat-leaf
  (Italian) parsley sprigs, tied in a bunch
3 tomatoes, peeled, seeded (page 48)
  and chopped
3 carrots, cut into chunks
4 zucchini (courgettes), cut into chunks

200 g (7 oz/1½ cups) shelled green peas
  or very young broad (fava) beans

COUSCOUS
1 quantity couscous (pages 248–9)
3 tablespoons herbed smen (page 247)
  or butter
420 g (15 oz) tin chickpeas, rinsed and
  drained
3 teaspoons harissa (page 250),
  or to taste

Serves 6–8

Joint the chicken into eight pieces (page 103). You don't need to remove the skin. Heat the smen in a large saucepan or the base of a large couscoussier, add the chicken and brown on each side. Reduce the heat, add the onion and cook until the onion has softened. Stir in the turmeric and cumin and add the onions. Pour in 750 ml (26 fl oz/3 cups) water, then add the saffron, cinnamon stick, the bunch of herbs and tomato. Season with 1½ teaspoons salt and freshly ground black pepper, to taste. Bring to a gentle boil, cover and cook over low heat for 25 minutes. Add the carrot and simmer for a further 20 minutes. Add the zucchini and green peas or broad beans and cook for 15–20 minutes, or until the chicken and vegetables are tender.

While the stew is cooking, prepare and steam the couscous as directed, either over the stew or over a saucepan of boiling water, or in the microwave oven. Stir the herbed smen through the couscous.

Heat the chickpeas in a saucepan with 3 tablespoons water, tossing them frequently, until the water evaporates. Add to the couscous and stir through.

Pile the couscous in a large, warm platter, make a dent in the centre and ladle the chicken and vegetables on top, letting some tumble down the sides. Moisten with some of the broth from the stew. Put 250 ml (9 fl oz/1 cup) of the broth into a bowl and stir in the harissa. The harissa-flavoured broth is added to the couscous to keep it moist, and according to individual taste.

couscous with chicken and vegetables

mechoui

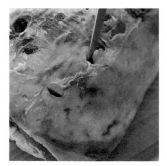

2.25 kg (5 lb) leg of lamb
70 g (2½ oz) butter, softened at
   room temperature
3 garlic cloves, crushed
2 teaspoons ground cumin
3 teaspoons ground coriander
1 teaspoon paprika
1 tablespoon ground cumin, extra,
   to serve
1½ teaspoons coarse salt, to serve

Serves 6

Preheat the oven to 220°C (425°F/Gas 7). With a small sharp knife, cut small deep slits in the top and sides of the lamb.

Mix the butter, garlic, spices and ¼ teaspoon salt in a bowl to form a smooth paste. With the back of a spoon, rub the paste all over the lamb, then use your fingers to spread the paste evenly, making sure all the lamb is covered.

Put the lamb, bone side down, in a deep roasting tin and place on the top shelf of the oven. Bake for 10 minutes, then baste the lamb and return it to the oven. Reduce the oven temperature to 160°C (315°F/Gas 2–3). Bake for 3¼ hours, basting every 20–30 minutes, to ensure the lamb stays tender and flavoursome. Carve the lamb into chunky pieces. Mix the extra cumin with the coarse salt and serve on the side for dipping.

4 x 175 g (6 oz) skinless, boneless
   chicken breasts
40 g (1½ oz) butter
1 teaspoon ground cinnamon
1 teaspoon ground ginger
¼ teaspoon freshly ground black pepper
⅛ teaspoon cayenne pepper
1 onion, sliced
250 ml (9 fl oz/1 cup) chicken stock
6 coriander (cilantro) sprigs,
   tied in a bunch
500 g (1 lb 2 oz) fresh apricots or
   425 g (15 oz) tin apricot halves, in
   natural juice
2 tablespoons honey
1 quantity couscous (pages 248–9)
2 tablespoons slivered almonds, toasted

Serves 4

Trim the chicken breasts of any fat or gristle. Melt the butter in a large frying pan. Add the spices and stir over low heat for 1 minute. Increase the heat to medium and add the chicken breasts. Turn them in the spiced butter and cook for 1 minute each side, without allowing the spices to burn.

Add the onion to the pan around the chicken and cook for 5 minutes, stirring the onion and turning the chicken occasionally. Add the chicken stock and coriander sprigs and season if necessary. Reduce the heat to low, cover and simmer for 5 minutes, turning the chicken once.

Wash and halve the apricots and remove the stones. Place them, cut side down, around the chicken and drizzle with honey. Cover and simmer for 7–8 minutes, turning the apricots after 5 minutes. Remove the chicken to a plate, cover and rest for 2–3 minutes. Slice each breast on the diagonal.

Prepare the couscous as directed, either using the steaming or microwave method. Put the hot couscous on serving plates and top each with sliced chicken. Remove the coriander sprigs from the sauce and spoon the sauce and apricots over the chicken. Scatter with the almonds and serve hot.

chicken with apricots and honey

tagine of beef with apples and raisins

1 kg (2 lb 4 oz) beef chuck steak
2 tablespoons oil
20 g (¾ oz) butter
1 onion, sliced
¼ teaspoon ground saffron threads
½ teaspoon ground ginger
1 teaspoon ground cinnamon
4 coriander (cilantro) sprigs, tied in a bunch

125 g (4½ oz/1 cup) raisins
3 tablespoons honey
3 tart apples, such as granny smiths
½ teaspoon ground cinnamon, extra
1 tablespoon sesame seeds, toasted

Serves 6

Trim the beef and cut it into 2.5 cm (1 in) cubes. In a heavy-based saucepan placed over high heat, add half the oil and half the butter and brown the beef in batches. Remove to a dish when cooked. Add the remaining oil as needed, and set aside the remaining butter.

Reduce the heat to medium, add the onion and cook gently for 5 minutes to soften. Sprinkle in the saffron, ginger and cinnamon and cook for 1 minute or so. Add 375 ml (13 fl oz/1½ cups) water, 1½ teaspoons salt and a generous grind of black pepper. Stir well and return the beef to the pan, along with the bunch of coriander sprigs. Cover and simmer over low heat for 1½ hours. Add the raisins and 1 tablespoon of the honey, then cover and simmer for a further 30 minutes, or until the meat is tender.

Meanwhile, wash the apples, halve and remove the cores. Cut each half into three wedges. Heat the remaining butter in a frying pan and add the apples. Cook for 10 minutes, turning the apples frequently. Drizzle with the remaining honey, dust with the extra cinnamon and cook for 5 minutes, or until glazed and softened.

Transfer the meat to a serving dish, pour the sauce over and arrange the apples on top. Serve hot, sprinkled with toasted sesame seeds.

1 kg (2 lb 4 oz) boneless lamb from
   shoulder or leg
30 g (1 oz) butter
1 onion, finely chopped
1 teaspoon ground ginger
1 teaspoon ground cinnamon
½ teaspoon freshly ground black pepper
55 g (2 oz/⅓ cup) pitted, chopped dried
   dates
pinch of ground saffron threads

2 tablespoons honey
2 tablespoons lemon juice
200 g (7 oz/1 cup) fresh or dessert dates
   (unpitted)
½ preserved lemon (page 251)
15 g (½ oz) butter, extra
40 g (1½ oz/⅓ cup) slivered almonds

Serves 6

Trim the lamb and cut it into 2.5 cm (1 in) cubes. In a large heavy-based saucepan, melt the butter over low heat, add the onion and cook gently until softened. Sprinkle in the ginger, cinnamon and black pepper and stir for 1 minute. Increase the heat to high, add the lamb and stir until the colour of the meat changes. Reduce the heat, add 375 ml (13 fl oz/1½ cups) water, the chopped dates, saffron and 1 teaspoon salt. Reduce the heat to low, cover and simmer for 1½ hours, stirring occasionally to prevent the sauce sticking as the chopped dates cook to a purée.

Stir in the honey and lemon juice and adjust the seasoning. Put the unpitted dates on top, cover and simmer for 10 minutes, or until the dates are plump.

Meanwhile, rinse the preserved lemon half under cold running water, remove and discard the pulp and membranes. Drain the rind, pat dry with paper towels and cut into strips. Melt the extra butter in a small frying pan, add the almonds and brown lightly, stirring often. Tip immediately onto a plate to prevent overbrowning.

Remove the whole dates from the top of the lamb and set them aside with the almonds. Ladle the meat into a serving dish or tagine and scatter the dates on top, along with the lemon strips and toasted almonds. Serve hot.

lamb tagine with dates

chicken with preserved lemon and olives

¼ **preserved lemon (page 251)**
3 **tablespoons olive oil**
1.6 **kg (3 lb 8 oz) chicken**
1 **onion, chopped**
2 **garlic cloves, chopped**
625 **ml (21½ fl oz/2½ cups) chicken stock**
½ **teaspoon ground ginger**
1½ **teaspoons ground cinnamon**
pinch of saffron threads
100 **g (3½ oz/½ cup) unpitted green**
   olives
2 **bay leaves**
2 **chicken livers**
3 **tablespoons chopped coriander**
   (cilantro) leaves

Serves 4

Rinse the preserved lemon quarter under cold running water, remove and discard the pulp and membranes. Drain the rind, pat dry with paper towels and cut into strips. Set aside.

Preheat the oven to 180°C (350°F/Gas 4). Heat 2 tablespoons of the olive oil in a large frying pan, add the chicken and brown on all sides. Place in a deep roasting tin.

Heat the remaining oil in the pan over medium heat, add the onion and garlic and cook for 3–4 minutes, or until the onion has softened. Add the chicken stock, ginger, cinnamon, saffron, olives, bay leaves and preserved lemon strips. Stir well, then pour the sauce around the chicken in the tin. Bake for 1½ hours, or until cooked through, adding a little more water or stock if the sauce gets too dry. Baste the chicken during cooking.

Remove the chicken from the tin, cover with foil and leave to rest. Pour the contents of the roasting tin into a frying pan, add the chicken livers and mash them into the sauce as they cook. Cook for 5–6 minutes, or until the sauce has reduced and thickened. Add the chopped coriander. Cut the chicken into four pieces and serve with the sauce.

60 g (2¼ oz) butter
3 lamb shanks
2 onions, quartered
½ teaspoon ground turmeric
1½ teaspoons ginger
1 teaspoon freshly ground black pepper
¼ teaspoon ground saffron threads
pinch of cayenne pepper

3 coriander (cilantro) sprigs and 3 flat-leaf
  (Italian) parsley sprigs, tied in a bunch
420 g (15 oz) tin chickpeas
1 onion, extra, halved and sliced
90 g (3¼ oz/¾ cup) raisins
1 quantity couscous (pages 248–9)

Serves 6–8

Heat the butter in a large saucepan or the base of a large couscoussier. Add the lamb shanks, onion quarters, turmeric, ginger, black pepper, saffron and cayenne pepper and stir over low heat for 1 minute. Add 500 ml (17 fl oz/ 2 cups) water, the bunch of herbs and 1 teaspoon salt. Bring to a gentle boil, cover and simmer over low heat for 1¾–2 hours, or until the lamb is tender.

Meanwhile, drain the chickpeas and put them in a large bowl with cold water to cover. Lift up handfuls of chickpeas and rub them between your hands to loosen the skins. Run more water into the bowl, stir well and let the skins float to the top, then skim them off. Repeat until all the skins have been removed. Drain and set aside.

When the lamb is cooked, lift the shanks from the broth to a dish and strip off the meat. Discard the bones and cut the meat into pieces. Return the meat to the pan, along with the chickpeas, extra sliced onion and the raisins. Cover and cook for 20 minutes, adding a little more water to the pan if necessary.

While the stew is cooking, prepare the couscous. Steam it either over the stew or over a saucepan of boiling water, or in the microwave oven.

Pile the couscous on a large, warm platter and make a dent in the centre. Remove and discard the herbs, then ladle the lamb mixture into the hollow. Moisten with some of the broth and put the remaining broth in a bowl, which can be added as needed.

couscous with lamb and raisins

lamb tagine
with quince

1.5 kg (3 lb 5 oz) lamb shoulder, cut into
   3 cm (1¼ in) pieces
2 large onions, diced
½ teaspoon ground ginger
½ teaspoon cayenne pepper
¼ teaspoon ground saffron threads
1 teaspoon ground coriander
1 cinnamon stick
2 large handfuls coriander (cilantro)
   leaves, roughly chopped
40 g (1½ oz) butter
500 g (1 lb 2 oz) quinces, peeled, cored
   and quartered
100 g (3½ oz/½ cup) dried apricots
1 tablespoon caster (superfine) sugar
coriander (cilantro) leaves, extra, to serve

Serves 4–6

Put the lamb in a heavy-based, flameproof casserole dish and add half the onion, the ginger, cayenne pepper, saffron, ground coriander, cinnamon stick, chopped coriander and some salt and pepper. Cover with cold water and bring to the boil over medium heat. Lower the heat and simmer, partly covered, for 1 hours.

While the lamb is cooking, melt the butter in a heavy-based frying pan and cook the remaining onion and the quinces for 15 minutes over medium heat, or until lightly golden. Add the quince mixture, apricots and sugar to the lamb and cook for 30 minutes, or until the lamb is tender.

Taste the sauce and adjust the seasoning if necessary. Transfer to a warm serving dish and sprinkle with the extra coriander. Serve with couscous or rice.

1.6 kg (3 lb 8 oz) chicken
2 teaspoons paprika
30 g (1 oz) butter, softened
250 ml (9 fl oz/1 cup) chicken stock

STUFFING
140 g (5 oz/¾ cup) couscous
40 g (1½ oz/⅓ cup) raisins
30 g (1 oz) butter, diced
1 tablespoon honey
½ teaspoon ground cinnamon
125 ml (4 fl oz/½ cup) boiling water
40 g (1½ oz/¼ cup) blanched almonds,
   lightly toasted

Serves 4–6

Preheat the oven to 180°C (350°F/Gas 4). Rinse the cavity of the chicken and dry with paper towels. Season the chicken on the outside and sprinkle with paprika. Rub it into the skin.

To prepare the stuffing, put the couscous in a glass or ceramic lidded casserole dish and mix in the raisins, butter, honey and cinnamon. Pour on the boiling water, stir well and set aside until the water has been absorbed. Fluff up the grains with a fork to break up the lumps, cover and microwave on full power for 2½ minutes. Fluff up again with the fork, add the almonds and toss through. Alternatively, follow the directions on the packet to prepare the couscous, adding the extra ingredients.

Spoon the stuffing into the cavity of the chicken, packing it in loosely. Tie the legs together and tuck the wing tips under.

Spread a little of the softened butter in the base of a roasting tin. Put the chicken, breast side up, in the tin, spread with the remaining butter and pour the stock into the tin. Roast for 1½–1¾ hours, basting often with the liquid in the pan. Remove to a platter and rest in a warm place for 15 minutes before carving. The juices left in the roasting tin may be strained over the chicken. Serve with orange and date salad (page 144) or orange and carrot salad (page 128).

roast chicken with couscous stuffing

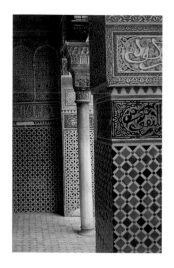

warkha... The pastry of the Maghreb, called *warkha* in Morocco, is tissue thin, made not by rolling out a dough, but by an intricate process that, these days, is usually left to the experts.

The dough is made with bread flour and water and, when rested, is divided into small balls. The *warkha* maker inverts a *tobsil*, a round, tinned copper pan, over a charcoal brazier in which the heat has been carefully controlled with ash (or steam). When heated, the *tobsil* is rubbed lightly with an oily cloth. A ball of sticky dough is rapidly rolled to-and-fro in the hand and tapped repeatedly onto the heated *tobsil*. This continues in a rhythmic way until the little dabs of dough join to form a complete sheet. When the dough is dry around the edges, it is peeled off. The process is so rapid that the sheet is made in a matter of seconds.

Knowing that a *bisteeya*, a pigeon or chicken pie, requires up to 40 sheets of pastry, one can appreciate why Moroccan cooks prefer to buy this pastry, and why restaurants employ a *warkha* maker. A true Moroccan *bisteeya* is fried in the *tobsil* (right side up), not baked, and frying a large *bisteeya* so that it is brown and crisp on each side takes considerable skill.

Warkha is believed to have come to Morocco with the Arabs and is Persian in origin. Its resemblance to the Chinese spring roll wrapper is more than coincidental. As the Persians had much contact with China in the days of the silk trade routes, and the Chinese spring roll wrappers were originally made in the same way (other methods are used now), it is entirely possible that its link is to China. Like spring roll wrappers, *warkha* must be fried — it cannot be baked or it toughens. Spring roll (and won ton) wrappers are excellent substitutes for fried dishes using *warkha*, such as briouats. Filo pastry is an ideal substitution in other recipes that traditionally would use *warkha*, and is recommended for *bisteeya*.

crisp pastries with almond cream

ALMOND CREAM
750 ml (26 fl oz/3 cups) milk
35 g (1¼ oz/¼ cup) cornflour (cornstarch)
60 g (2¼ oz/¼ cup) sugar
50 g (1¾ oz/½ cup) ground almonds
¼ teaspoon almond extract
1½ tablespoons rosewater

100 g (3½ oz/⅔ cup) blanched almonds,
  lightly toasted
2 tablespoons icing (confectioners') sugar,
  sifted, plus extra, to serve
½ teaspoon ground cinnamon
40 square won ton wrappers
oil, for frying
unsprayed rose petals, to serve

Serves 6

To make the almond cream, put 125 ml (4 fl oz/½ cup) of the milk in a large bowl, add the cornflour and mix to a thin paste. Bring the remaining milk to the boil until it froths up. Mix the cornflour paste again, then pour in the boiling milk, mixing constantly with a balloon whisk. Pour this back into the saucepan and stir in the sugar and ground almonds. Return to the heat; stir constantly with a wooden spoon until thickened and bubbling. Reduce the heat and boil gently for 1 minute. Pour back into the bowl and stir in the almond extract and rosewater. Press a piece of plastic wrap on the surface and leave to cool. Just before using the cream, stir briskly with a balloon whisk to smooth it; if it is too thick, stir in a little milk to give a pouring consistency.

Roughly chop the toasted almonds, mix with the icing sugar and cinnamon, and set aside. Bring the won ton wrappers to room temperature. Lightly brush a wrapper with water and press another firmly on top. Repeat until there are 18 pairs. Make two extra pairs in case some are burnt when frying.

In a large frying pan, add oil to a depth of 1 cm (½ in) and place over high heat. When the oil is hot, but not smoking, reduce the heat to medium and add two pairs of won ton wrappers. Fry for about 20 seconds until lightly browned, turning to brown evenly. Using tongs, remove the wrappers and drain on paper towels. Repeat with the remaining squares.

To assemble the pastries, put a fried pastry square in the centre of each plate. Drizzle with a little almond cream and sprinkle with a heaped teaspoon of the chopped almond mixture. Repeat with another pastry square, cream and almonds. Finish with another pastry square. Scatter with pink rose petals from roses that have not been sprayed. Sift a little icing sugar over the top and serve with the remaining almond cream in a pitcher.

12 fresh purple-skinned figs
50 g (1¾ oz/⅓ cup) blanched almonds,
  lightly toasted
3–4 teaspoons rosewater
1–2 tablespoons honey

Serves 6

Wash the figs gently and pat them dry with paper towels. Cut each fig into quarters, starting from the stem end and cutting almost to the base, then gently open out and put on a serving platter. Cover and chill in the refrigerator for 1 hour, or until required.

Roughly chop the toasted almonds and set aside.

Carefully dribble about ¼ teaspoon of the rosewater onto the exposed centres of each of the figs, and sprinkle 1 teaspoon of the chopped almonds into each fig. Drizzle a little honey over the nuts. Serve immediately.

figs with rosewater, almonds and honey

sweet couscous

80 g (2¾ oz) combined pistachio nuts,
  pine nuts and blanched almonds
40 g (1½ oz/¼ cup) dried apricots
250 g (9 oz/1⅓ cups) couscous
55 g (2 oz/¼ cup) caster (superfine) sugar
250 ml (9 fl oz/1 cup) boiling water
90 g (3¼ oz) unsalted butter, softened
2 tablespoons caster (superfine) sugar,
  extra
½ teaspoon ground cinnamon
375 ml (13 fl oz/1½ cups) hot milk

Serves 4–6

Preheat the oven to 160°C (315°F/Gas 2–3). Spread the nuts on a baking tray and bake for about 5 minutes, or until lightly golden. Allow to cool, then roughly chop and place in a bowl. Slice the apricots into matchstick-sized pieces. Add to the bowl with the nuts and toss to combine.

Put the couscous and sugar in a large bowl and cover with the boiling water. Stir well, then add the butter and a pinch of salt. Stir until the butter melts. Cover with a tea towel (dish towel) and set aside for 10 minutes. (Alternatively, you can prepare and steam or microwave the couscous as described on pages 248–9.) Fluff the grains with a fork, then toss through half the fruit and nut mixture.

To serve, pile the warm couscous in the centre of a platter. Arrange the remaining nut mixture around the edge. Combine the extra sugar and the cinnamon in a small bowl and serve separately for sprinkling. Pass around the hot milk in a jug for guests to help themselves.

a little taste of...

With both the Atlantic Ocean and Mediterranean Sea lapping its coastline, Morocco has an abundance of seafood. Most of the fish is exported, and little reaches inland where freshwater fish is used. Instead, Moroccans travel to the seaside to enjoy the delights on offer. And they are many — anchovies, sardines, bluefish, tuna, turbot, swordfish, sole, sea bream, red mullet, whiting, mackerel and monkfish are displayed on slabs of concrete, splashed frequently with seawater to keep them fresh. Lobster, prawns (shrimp) and sea urchins, clams, squid, mussels and oysters add colour. Fish fried in a saffron-coloured batter with fried slices of eggplant (aubergine) and potato chips on the side is standard street food at the seaside. Add to this many stalls with displays of seafood ready for cooking on charcoal fires, picnic tables for eating in comfort and a few good restaurants, and seafood lovers can rejoice. The coast dwellers contribute their recipes to Morocco's table — fragrant fish tagines, fabulous stuffed fish, and fish balls introduced by the Jewish community.

...the coast

fish soup

2 red capsicums (peppers)
1 long red chilli
2 tablespoons extra virgin olive oil
1 onion, finely chopped
1 tablespoon tomato paste
   (concentrated purée)
2–3 teaspoons harissa (page 250),
   to taste
4 garlic cloves, finely chopped
2 teaspoons ground cumin

750 ml (26 fl oz/3 cups) fish stock
400 g (14 oz) tin chopped tomatoes
750 g (1 lb 10 oz) firm white fish, such
   as blue eye cod or ling, cut into 2 cm
   (¾ in) cubes
2 bay leaves
2 tablespoons chopped coriander
   (cilantro) leaves

Serves 6

Cut the capsicums into quarters and remove the membrane and seeds. Cut the chilli in half and remove the seeds. Place the capsicum and chilli pieces, skin side up, under a grill (broiler) and grill (broil) until the skin blackens. Remove and place in a plastic bag, tuck the end of the bag underneath and leave to steam in the bag until cool enough to handle. Remove the blackened skin from the capsicum and the chilli and cut into thin strips. Set aside.

Heat the oil in a large saucepan and cook the onion for 5 minutes, or until softened. Add the tomato paste, harissa, garlic, cumin and 125 ml (4 fl oz/ ½ cup) water, then stir to combine. Add the fish stock, tomatoes and 500 ml (17 fl oz/2 cups) water. Bring to the boil, then reduce the heat and add the fish and bay leaves. Simmer for 7–8 minutes, or until the fish is just done.

Remove the fish with a slotted spoon and place on a plate. Discard the bay leaves. When the soup has cooled slightly, add half the chopped coriander and purée in a blender until smooth. Season with salt and pepper.

Return the soup to the pan, add the fish, capsicum and chilli and simmer gently for 5 minutes. Garnish with the remaining coriander and serve hot with crusty bread.

800 g (1 lb 12 oz) tuna steaks, cut into
   3 cm (1¼ in) cubes
2 tablespoons olive oil
½ teaspoon ground cumin
2 teaspoons finely grated lemon zest

CHERMOULA
½ teaspoon ground coriander
3 teaspoons ground cumin
2 teaspoons paprika

pinch of cayenne pepper
4 garlic cloves, crushed
3 tablespoons chopped flat-leaf
   (Italian) parsley
3 tablespoons chopped coriander
   (cilantro) leaves
80 ml (2½ fl oz/⅓ cup) lemon juice
125 ml (4 fl oz/½ cup) olive oil

Serves 4

Soak eight bamboo skewers in water for 2 hours, or use metal skewers.

Put the tuna in a shallow non-metallic dish. Combine the olive oil, cumin and lemon zest and pour over the tuna. Toss to coat, then cover and marinate in the refrigerator for 10 minutes.

Meanwhile, to make the chermoula, put the ground coriander, cumin, paprika and cayenne pepper in a small frying pan and cook over medium heat for 30 seconds, or until fragrant. Combine with the remaining chermoula ingredients and set aside.

Thread the tuna onto the skewers. Lightly oil a chargrill pan or barbecue grill and cook the skewers for 1 minute on each side for rare, or 2 minutes for medium. Serve with the chermoula drizzled over the tuna.

tuna skewers
with chermoula

a fish tagine... When Moroccan cooks want to impress with their cooking skills, they prefer to make a fish tagine, rather than to cook the fish over the charcoal. The fish is left whole though the head and tail may be removed if the fish is too large for the tagine. There are many wonderful combinations of

ingredients — herbs, onions, garlic and spices; dried dates, raisins or prunes with onions and spices; tomatoes and fennel stalks; or tomatoes, potatoes and green capsicums (peppers). The fish may be prepared in many ways — first coated with ground almonds, then stuffed with dates or prunes; or prepared with eggs, onion and preserved lemons, sometimes seasoned with a little cinnamon.

Before the advent of the oven in Moroccan homes, something which is still considered a luxury today, the Moroccan cook had a special way in which to cook a whole fish in a tagine so that it wouldn't stick to the base of the pot. Thin bamboo canes are crisscrossed in the base and the fish is placed on top with its sauce and embellishments. Variations on the theme include the use of short lengths of celery or carrot batons, or a layer of onion or potato, which then becomes part of the dish. The fish is presented at the table in the tagine. This is where eating with the fingers comes into its own. When morsels are delicately plucked from the fish, bones can be easily felt and left behind, and the fish tastes so much better because it is untainted by metal cutlery.

trout stuffed
with dates

4 medium-sized trout
140 g (5 oz/¾ cup) pitted, chopped
   dried dates
40 g (1½ oz/¼ cup) cooked rice
4 tablespoons chopped coriander
   (cilantro) leaves
¼ teaspoon ground ginger
¼ teaspoon ground cinnamon
50 g (1¾ oz/⅓ cup) roughly chopped
   blanched almonds
1 onion, finely chopped
40 g (1½ oz) butter, softened
ground cinnamon, to serve

Serves 4

Preheat the oven to 180°C (350°F/Gas 4). Rinse the trout under cold running water and pat them dry with paper towels. Season lightly with salt and pepper.

Combine the dates, cooked rice, coriander, ginger, cinnamon, almonds, half the onion and half the butter in a bowl. Season well with salt and pepper.

Spoon the stuffing into the fish cavities and place each fish on a well-greased double sheet of foil. Brush the fish with the remaining butter, season with salt and pepper and divide the remaining onion among the four parcels. Wrap the fish neatly and seal the edges of the foil. Place the parcels on a large baking tray and bake for 15–20 minutes, or until cooked to your liking. Serve dusted with cinnamon.

**375 g (13 oz) raw medium prawns
   (shrimp)**
3 tablespoons olive oil
½ teaspoon ground cumin
½ teaspoon cumin seeds
1 teaspoon ground ginger
2 teaspoons chopped red chilli
3 garlic cloves, finely chopped
½ teaspoon ground turmeric
1 teaspoon paprika
**2 tablespoons finely chopped coriander
   (cilantro) leaves**
lemon wedges, to serve

Serves 4

Peel the prawns, leaving the tails intact. To devein the prawns, cut a slit down the back and remove any visible vein. Put the prawns in a colander and rinse under cold running water. Shake the colander to remove any excess water, sprinkle the prawns with ½ teaspoon salt, toss through and set aside.

Pour the olive oil into a large frying pan and place over medium heat. Stir in the ground cumin, cumin seeds, ginger and chilli. Cook until fragrant and the cumin seeds start to pop, then add the garlic, turmeric and paprika. Cook, stirring, for a few seconds, then add the prawns. Increase the heat a little and fry the prawns, tossing frequently, for 3–4 minutes until they firm up and turn pink. Stir in the coriander and 3 tablespoons water, bring to a simmer and remove from the heat. Serve immediately with lemon wedges.

spicy prawns

fish with
harissa and olives

80 ml (2½ fl oz/⅓ cup) olive oil
4 firm white fish fillets, such as blue eye
   cod, snapper or perch
seasoned plain (all-purpose) flour, to dust
1 onion, chopped
2 garlic cloves, crushed
400 g (14 oz) tin chopped tomatoes
2 teaspoons harissa (page 250),
   or to taste
2 bay leaves
1 cinnamon stick
185 g (6½ oz/1 cup) black olives
1 tablespoon lemon juice
2 tablespoons chopped flat-leaf
   (Italian) parsley

Serves 4

Heat half the olive oil in a heavy-based frying pan. Dust the fish fillets with the flour and cook over medium heat for 2 minutes on each side, or until golden. Transfer to a plate.

Add the remaining olive oil to the pan and cook the onion and garlic for 3–4 minutes, or until softened. Add the tomatoes, harissa, bay leaves and cinnamon stick. Cook for 10 minutes, or until the sauce has thickened. Season, to taste, with salt and freshly ground black pepper.

Return the fish to the pan, add the olives and cover the fish with the sauce. Remove the bay leaves and cinnamon stick and cook for 2 minutes, or until the fish is tender. Add the lemon juice and parsley and serve.

24 fresh sardines
olive oil, for frying
plain (all-purpose) flour, to dust
lemon wedges, to serve

STUFFING
1 tablespoon drained grated onion
1 garlic clove, crushed
3 tablespoons finely chopped flat-leaf
   (Italian) parsley
3 tablespoons finely chopped coriander
   (cilantro) leaves

¼ teaspoon cayenne pepper
½ teaspoon paprika
¼ teaspoon freshly ground black pepper
½ teaspoon ground cumin
½ teaspoon grated lemon zest
2 teaspoons lemon juice
2 teaspoons olive oil

Serves 6 as an appetizer

To **butterfly** the sardines, first remove the heads. Cut through the undersides of the sardines and rinse under cold running water. Snip the backbone at the tail with kitchen scissors, without cutting through the skin, and pull carefully away from body starting from the tail end. Open out the sardines and pat the inside surface dry with paper towels and sprinkle lightly with salt. Set aside.

To **make** the stuffing, put the drained onion in a bowl and add the garlic, parsley, coriander, cayenne pepper, paprika, black pepper, cumin, lemon zest and juice and olive oil. Mix well.

Place 12 sardines on the work surface, skin side down. Spread the stuffing evenly on each sardine and cover with another sardine, skin side up. Press them firmly together.

Heat the olive oil to a depth of 5 mm (¼ in) in a large frying pan. Dust the sardines with flour and fry in the hot oil for 2 minutes on each side, or until crisp and evenly browned. Serve hot with lemon wedges.

stuffed sardines

fish tagine with tomato and potato

CHERMOULA
2 garlic cloves, roughly chopped
3 tablespoons chopped flat-leaf (Italian)
   parsley
3 tablespoons chopped
   coriander (cilantro) leaves
2 teaspoons paprika
2 teaspoons ground cumin
¼ teaspoon cayenne pepper
1 tablespoon lemon juice
2 tablespoons olive oil

4 x 2 cm (¾ in) thick firm white fish
   steaks, such as snapper or blue eye cod
500 g (1 lb 2 oz) potatoes
375 g (13 oz) ripe tomatoes
1 green capsicum (pepper)
1½ tablespoons tomato paste
   (concentrated purée)
1 teaspoon sugar
1 tablespoon lemon juice
2 tablespoons olive oil
2 tablespoons combined chopped flat-leaf
   (Italian) parsley and coriander (cilantro)
   leaves

Serves 4

To make the chermoula, pound the garlic to a paste with ½ teaspoon salt using a mortar and pestle. Add the parsley, coriander, paprika, cumin, cayenne pepper and lemon juice. Pound the mixture to a rough paste and then work in the olive oil.

Rub half the chermoula on each side of the fish, place the fish in a dish, then cover and set aside for 20 minutes.

Cut the potatoes and tomatoes into 5 mm (¼ in) thick slices. Remove the seeds and white membranes from the capsicum and cut into 5 mm (¼ in) thick strips. Preheat the oven to 200°C (400°F/Gas 6).

Brush a 30 x 40 x 6 cm (12 x 16 x 2½ in) ovenproof dish with oil. Place a layer of potato slices in the bottom. Put the fish on top. Toss the remaining potato slices with the remaining chermoula and arrange over the fish. Top with the tomato and capsicum strips. Mix the tomato paste with 125 ml (4 fl oz/½ cup) water and add ½ teaspoon salt, a good grinding of black pepper, the sugar, lemon juice and olive oil. Pour over the fish and sprinkle with the mixed herbs.

Cover the dish with foil and bake in the oven for 40 minutes, then remove the foil and move the dish to the upper shelf. Cook for a further 10 minutes, or until the fish and potato are tender and the top is lightly crusted. Serve hot.

4 x 200 g (7 oz) firm white fish fillets,
　such as blue eye cod, snapper, hake or
　sea bass
24 pitted prunes
24 blanched almonds, lightly toasted
30 g (1 oz) butter
2 onions, sliced
¾ teaspoon ground ginger
¾ teaspoon ground cinnamon
⅛ teaspoon freshly ground black pepper

⅛ teaspoon ground saffron threads
1½ teaspoons sugar
3 teaspoons lemon juice
3 teaspoons orange flower water
1 egg
100 g (3½ oz/1 cup) ground almonds
3–4 tablespoons smen (page 247) or ghee
lemon wedges, to serve

Serves 4

Choose centre-cut fish fillets no more than 3 cm (1¼ in) thick at the thickest part. Remove the skin (if present) and season lightly with salt. Set aside. Stuff each prune with a whole toasted almond and set aside.

Melt the butter in a frying pan and add the onion. Cook for 10 minutes over low heat, stirring often, until the onion is soft and golden. Add ½ teaspoon each of the ground ginger and cinnamon, a pinch of salt and the black pepper. Stir and cook for a few seconds. Pour in 250 ml (9 fl oz/1 cup) water and stir in the saffron. Cover and simmer gently for 5 minutes, then add the stuffed prunes, sugar, lemon juice and orange flower water and stir gently. Cover and simmer for 15 minutes, or until the prunes are plump.

Meanwhile, beat the egg in a shallow dish with ¼ teaspoon each of ground ginger, cinnamon and salt. Spread the ground almonds in a flat dish. Dip the fish into the beaten egg, drain briefly, and coat on all sides with the ground almonds. Place on a tray lined with baking paper.

Melt the smen in a large non-stick frying pan over medium to high heat (the depth of the smen should be about 5 mm/¼ in). Add the coated fish, reduce the heat to medium and cook for 2 minutes, then turn and cook for a further 2 minutes, or until golden and just cooked through. Do not allow the almond coating to burn. If you have to remove the fish before it is cooked through, place it on top of the onion and prune mixture, cover and simmer gently for 2–3 minutes, taking care that the coating does not become too moist on top. Serve the fish immediately with the onion and prune sauce, with a lemon wedge to squeeze over the fish.

almond-crusted
fish with prunes

prawns in
chermoula

1 kg (2 lb 4 oz) raw large prawns
(shrimp)
2 tablespoons olive oil
lemon wedges, to serve
saffron rice (page 246), to serve

CHERMOULA
½ preserved lemon (page 251)
2 garlic cloves, roughly chopped
3 tablespoons chopped flat-leaf
(Italian) parsley
3 tablespoons chopped coriander
(cilantro) leaves

¼ teaspoon ground saffron threads
(optional)
½ teaspoon paprika
⅛–¼ teaspoon cayenne pepper,
or ½ teaspoon harissa (page 250),
or to taste
½ teaspoon ground cumin
2 tablespoons lemon juice
3 tablespoons olive oil

Serves 4

Peel the prawns, leaving the tails intact. To devein the prawns, cut a slit down the back and remove any visible vein. Place the prawns in a colander and rinse under cold running water. Shake the colander to remove any excess water, sprinkle the prawns with the salt, toss through and set aside.

To make the chermoula, remove the pulp and membrane from the preserved lemon, rinse the rind and pat dry. Chop roughly and place in a food processor bowl, along with the garlic, parsley, coriander, saffron (if using), paprika, cayenne pepper or harissa, cumin and lemon juice. Process to a coarse paste, gradually adding the olive oil while processing.

Heat the olive oil in a large frying pan over medium–high heat, then add the prawns and cook, stirring often, until they begin to turn pink. Reduce the heat to medium, add the chermoula and continue to cook, stirring often, for 3 minutes, or until the prawns are firm. Serve hot with lemon wedges and saffron rice.

chermoula...

Also transliterated as *t'chermila*, this marinade and sauce is indispensable for cooking fish. It is usually made from a combination of fresh coriander (cilantro), flat-leaf (Italian) parsley, garlic, onion, cumin, ground coriander seeds, saffron, paprika and cayenne pepper, but the ingredients may vary slightly according to the cook and the food it is to partner. Preserved lemon may sometimes be added, or lemon juice or vinegar — it all depends on the cook's preference.

When using chermoula as a marinade for fish, the fish is marinated for only a short time if the chermoula contains lemon juice in quantities greater than 1 or 2 teaspoons, as the lemon juice can actually 'cook' the fish. The fish is then placed in a wire basket and cooked over a glowing charcoal fire, and basted with the marinade. A small amount of the marinade is often reserved and used as a sauce when serving the fish.

Chermoula is also used in fish tagines, and prawns and squid both marry well with this herb and spice mix, especially if it contains preserved lemon. It is also very good with mussels — the chermoula is cooked in a large saucepan for a minute or so, the scrubbed mussels are added, then the pot is covered and the mussels left to cook until they open. Chermoula can serve as a marinade for chicken and lamb, but without the saffron added to the mixture. It is also an excellent marinade for olives.

500 g (1 lb 2 oz) boneless firm white
   fish fillets
1 egg
2 spring onions (scallions), chopped
1 tablespoon chopped flat-leaf
   (Italian) parsley
1 tablespoon chopped coriander
   (cilantro) leaves
55 g (2 oz/⅔ cup) fresh breadcrumbs
⅛ teaspoon ground saffron threads

TOMATO SAUCE
500 g (1 lb 2 oz) tomatoes
1 onion, coarsely grated
3 tablespoons olive oil
2 garlic cloves, finely chopped
1 teaspoon paprika
½ teaspoon harissa (page 250), or to
   taste, or ¼ teaspoon cayenne pepper
½ teaspoon ground cumin
1 teaspoon sugar

Serves 4

Cut the fish fillets into rough pieces and put in a food processor bowl, along with the egg, spring onion, parsley, coriander and breadcrumbs. Mix the saffron in 1 tablespoon warm water and add to the other ingredients with ¾ teaspoon salt and some freshly ground black pepper. Process to a thick paste, scraping down the sides of the bowl occasionally.

With moistened hands, shape the fish mixture into balls the size of a walnut. Put on a tray, cover and set aside in the refrigerator.

To make the tomato sauce, first peel the tomatoes by scoring a cross in the base of each one. Put them in a bowl of boiling water for 20 seconds, then plunge into a bowl of cold water to cool. Remove from the water and peel the skin away from the cross—it should slip off easily. Halve the tomatoes crossways and squeeze out the seeds. Chop the tomatoes and set aside.

Put the onion and olive oil in a saucepan and cook over medium heat for 5 minutes. Add the garlic, paprika, harissa or cayenne pepper, and cumin. Stir for a few seconds, then add the tomato, sugar, 250 ml (9 fl oz/1 cup) water, and salt and freshly ground pepper, to taste. Bring to the boil, cover and simmer for 15 minutes.

Add the fish balls to the tomato sauce, shaking the pan occasionally as they are added so that they settle into the sauce. Return to a gentle boil over medium heat, then cover and reduce the heat to low. Simmer for 20 minutes. Serve hot with crusty bread.

saffron fish balls in tomato sauce

a little taste of...

The village cafés of Morocco owe more to Middle Eastern culture than to any French influence: that is, they are meeting places for men. Moroccan males sit at the outdoor tables, sipping glasses of mint tea or strong black French-style coffee; in a few cafés Turkish-style coffee is available. Moroccan women are seldom seen here, but young girls are permitted to go in company to the cafés that have indoor seating. In the cities, cafés approach the French model and cater to tourists. They serve breakfasts — a baguette or bread with butter and jam, or *beghrir*, semolina pancakes; and lunches — tagines, salads, kebabs and couscous served alongside sandwiches and pizzas. Also available are fresh fruit and vegetable juices, very sweet yoghurt and *sharbats*, often made with apple or avocado (don't ask for avocado to be added to your salad or baguette sandwich, as this is a strange concept to most Moroccans). It is quite in order to purchase fresh doughnuts or sweet pastries from a patisserie and to take them to the café to have with your mint tea.

...caf´ life

mint tea

**1 tablespoon Chinese green tea leaves
    (preferably Gunpowder green tea)**
1½ tablespoons sugar
**large handful spearmint leaves and stalks,
    plus extra sprigs, to garnish**

Serves 4

Heat the teapot and add the green tea leaves, the sugar and spearmint leaves and stalks. Fill with boiling water and brew for at least 3 minutes. Adjust the sweetness if necessary.

This light sweet tea is often served before, and always after, every meal, and is prepared at any hour of the day when friends or guests arrive at a Moroccan home. It is sipped in cafés. Traditionally it is poured from a silver teapot into ornately painted glasses.

1 small egg, separated
200 g (7 oz/2 cups) ground almonds
30 g (1 oz/⅓ cup) flaked almonds
125 g (4½ oz/1 cup) icing (confectioners') sugar
1 teaspoon finely grated lemon zest
¼ teaspoon almond extract
1 tablespoon rosewater

90 g (3¼ oz) unsalted butter or smen, melted
8–9 sheets filo pastry
pinch of ground cinnamon
icing (confectioners') sugar, extra, to serve

Serves 8

Preheat the oven to 180°C (350°F/Gas 4). Lightly grease a 20 cm (8 in) round springform tin.

Put the egg white in a bowl and beat lightly with a fork. Add the ground almonds and flaked almonds, the icing sugar, lemon zest, almond extract and rosewater. Mix to a paste.

Divide the mixture into four and roll each portion on a cutting board into a sausage shape about 5 cm (2 in) shorter than the length of filo pastry (about 38 cm (15 in) long) and 1 cm (½ in) thick. If the paste is too sticky to roll, dust the cutting board with icing sugar.

Keep the melted butter warm by placing the saucepan in another pan filled with hot water. Remove one sheet of filo pastry and place the rest in the folds of a dry tea towel (dish towel) or cover them with plastic wrap to prevent them from drying out. Brush the filo sheet with the butter, then cover with another sheet of filo, brushing the top with butter. Ease one almond 'sausage' off the board onto the buttered pastry, laying it along the length of the pastry, 2.5 cm (1 in) in from the base and sides. Roll up to enclose the filling. Form into a coil and sit the coil, seam side down, in the centre of the tin, tucking under the unfilled ends of the pastry to enclose the filling. Continue in this manner to make more pastry 'snakes', shaping to make a large coil. If the coil breaks, cut small pieces of remaining filo sheet, brush with a little egg yolk and press the filo onto the breaks.

Add the cinnamon to the remaining egg yolk and brush over the coil. Bake for 30–35 minutes, or until golden brown. Dust with the extra icing sugar and serve warm. This sweet pastry can be stored at room temperature for up to 2 days.

almond filo coil

sesame biscuits

225 g (8 oz/1½ cups) sesame seeds
125 g (4½ oz/1 cup) plain (all-purpose)
   flour, sifted
165 g (5¾ oz/¾ cup) caster (superfine)
   sugar
1½ teaspoons baking powder
2 eggs, beaten
1 tablespoon orange flower water
2–3 tablespoons sesame seeds, extra

Makes about 36

Put the sesame seeds in a heavy-based saucepan and stir constantly over medium heat until golden—about 7 minutes. Tip them immediately into a bowl and leave to cool. Put the flour in the same saucepan, stir constantly over medium heat for about 5 minutes, or until lightly golden, then transfer immediately to a mixing bowl.

When the sesame seeds are cool, put them in a blender and process until reduced almost to a powder (this is best done in two batches as it is difficult to process the seeds efficiently in one batch). Some seeds should remain visible after processing. Add to the flour, along with the caster sugar and baking powder and mix thoroughly. Make a well in the centre and add the beaten eggs and orange flower water. Stir into the dry ingredients, then knead well until smooth.

Put the extra sesame seeds in a shallow dish. Line two baking trays with baking paper or grease them well with butter. Preheat the oven to 180°C (350°F/Gas 4).

Break off pieces of dough the size of a walnut and roll it into balls, oiling your hands lightly to prevent the dough sticking. Press the balls in the extra sesame seeds and flatten slightly. Lift carefully so that the topping is not disturbed and place, sesame side up, on the baking trays, spacing them 5 cm (2 in) apart to allow for spreading. Bake for 15–20 minutes, or until golden. Leave on the trays for 10 minutes before removing to a wire rack to cool. Store in an airtight container.

200 g (7 oz/2 cups) ground almonds
90 g (3¼ oz) unsalted butter
60 g (2¼ oz/½ cup) icing (confectioners')
   sugar
¼ teaspoon almond extract
2 tablespoons orange flower water

6 sheets filo pastry
125 g (4½ oz) smen (page 247), melted
260 g (9¼ oz/¾ cup) honey

Makes 18

Heat a heavy-based saucepan, add the ground almonds and stir constantly until lightly toasted—about 3–4 minutes. Tip immediately into a bowl. Add the butter to the pan and stir until melted. When cool, add the icing sugar, almond extract and 1 tablespoon of the orange flower water. Mix thoroughly to a paste.

Stack the filo sheets on a cutting board with the longer side towards you and, with a ruler and sharp knife, measure and cut into strips 11 cm (4¼ in) wide and 28–30 cm (11¼–12 in) long. Stack the strips in the folds of a tea towel (dish towel) or cover with plastic wrap to prevent them from drying out.

Place a filo strip on the work surface, brush half the length with the smen and fold it in half to give a strip 5.5 cm (2¼ in) wide. Brush over the top with the smen and place a heaped tablespoon of the almond filling towards the end of the strip. Fold the end diagonally across the filling so that the base lines up with the side of the strip, forming a triangle. Fold straight up once, then fold diagonally to the opposite side. Complete folding in the same manner to the end of the strip, trimming any excess pastry with scissors. Place, seam side down, on a lightly greased baking tray. Repeat with the remaining ingredients and when completed, brush the tops lightly with the smen.

Preheat the oven to 180°C (350°F/Gas 4). It is best to do this after the triangles are completed so that the kitchen remains cool during shaping. Bake the pastries for 20–25 minutes, or until puffed and lightly golden.

Combine the honey, 3 tablespoons water and remaining orange flower water in a 1.5 litre (52 fl oz/6 cup) saucepan. Just before the pastries are removed from the oven, bring the honey to the boil and reduce the heat to low. Put two hot pastries at a time in the boiling honey, leave for 20 seconds and remove with two forks to a tray lined with baking paper. Dip the remainder in the same way, placing them on the tray, right side up. As the pastries are dipped, the honey boils up in the pan, so take care. Cool and serve on the day of baking.

honey-dipped briouats with almond paste

mint tea... Most of the herbs used in cooking today are indigenous to the Mediterranean region and the Middle East. Because of their perceived health benefits, herbal infusions have always been popular, long before tea and coffee were 'discovered'. That is how it was in Morocco, and as mint grows there particularly well, especially in the Atlas Mountains, mint tea was taken for indigestion and as a calmative.

In 1854, during the Crimean War, British tea merchants were forced to look for new markets because of embargoes, and they found them in Tangier and Mogador. The Moroccans embraced tea drinking with much enthusiasm, and soon found that the pale greenish brew perfectly complemented their favoured mint infusion.

The preferred tea is a green tea called Gunpowder. The teapot is similar to that of the British 'Manchester' in shape, with a bulbous body and a domed lid. It is made in silver plate, aluminium or stainless steel. Highly refined loaf sugar must be used for the best results. This sugar is shaped in cones about 20 cm (8 in) high, which are wrapped in purple paper (or plastic). Spearmint (*Mentha spicata* or *M. viridis*) is the preferred mint. The tea and the sugar lumps, which are broken from the loaf, are put into the pot, boiling water is added, then well-washed mint sprigs are packed into the pot. It is left to brew for 3 minutes. The first glass is poured, then returned to

the pot to mix the brew, then poured into the tea glasses from a height, which helps to aerate the tea. When the head of the house pours the tea after a formal meal, this takes on the form of ceremony, and is sometimes poured from two teapots for maximum effect and aeration. Guests are expected to have three glasses of the tea.

Tea is omnipresent — it may be drunk at any time of the day in the home, in cafés, brewed by workers in the fields, or thrust into your hand when bargaining for a carpet or a piece of jewellery. And how do you drink tea from a glass? Grip the rim of the glass with the thumb and forefinger of the right hand and sip, sip, sip...

almond sharbat

235 g (8½ oz/1½ cups) blanched almonds
55 g (2 oz/¼ cup) caster (superfine) sugar
¼ teaspoon almond extract
½ teaspoon rosewater
250 ml (9 fl oz/1 cup) cold milk

Serves 4

Put the almonds and sugar in a blender with 250 ml (9 fl oz/1 cup) water. Blend until the almonds are well pulverized.

Line a strainer with a double layer of muslin (cheesecloth), place over a bowl and pour the almond mixture into the strainer. Add 3 tablespoons water to the blender and blend briefly to clean the blender of any almond residue. Pour into the strainer. Press the almonds to extract as much moisture as possible, gather up the muslin, twist the end and squeeze firmly over the bowl, taking care that the almonds are safely enclosed. Place the muslin and almonds in the strainer again, add another 3 tablespoons water, stir and squeeze the almonds again. Discard the almonds.

Stir in the almond extract, rosewater and milk, taste and add a little more sugar if necessary. Chill and serve. (If you can find them, float a fragrant pink rose petal or two on top of each, but ensure the petals are free of pesticides.)

150 g (5½ oz/1½ cups) walnut halves
2 tablespoons sesame seeds
100 g (3½ oz) smen (page 247) or ghee
600 g (1 lb 5 oz/13⅓ cups) pitted dried
   dates, roughly chopped

Serves 6–8

Preheat the oven to 180°C (350°F/Gas 4) and line the base of an 18 cm
(7 in) square baking tin with baking paper. Spread the walnuts on a baking
tray and bake for 5 minutes, or until lightly toasted. Chop roughly. Bake the
sesame seeds on a tray until golden.

Melt the smen in a large heavy-based saucepan and cook the dates, covered,
over low heat for about 10 minutes, stirring often, until the dates soften. Using
the back of a spoon dipped in cold water, spread half the dates over the
base of the tin. Scatter the walnuts on top and press into the dates. Spread
the remaining date mixture over the walnuts. Smooth the surface with wet
fingers and press down firmly.

Sprinkle with the sesame seeds and press lightly into the dates. When cool,
remove the set mixture from the tin and cut into small diamonds to serve.

date candies

gazelle's horns

PASTRY
300 g (10½ oz/2½ cups) plain
 (all-purpose) flour
20 g (¾ oz) butter, melted
1 egg yolk
2 tablespoons orange flower water

ALMOND FILLING
90 g (3¼ oz/¾ cup) icing (confectioners')
 sugar, plus extra, to dust

300 g (10½ oz/3 cups) ground almonds
1 tablespoon orange flower water
1 egg white, lightly beaten
40 g (1½ oz) unsalted butter, melted
½ teaspoon ground cinnamon
¼ teaspoon almond extract

Makes about 30

To make the pastry, put the flour in the food processor bowl with the melted butter, egg yolk, orange flower water and 3 tablespoons cold water. Process until the dough forms on the blades, adding a little more water if necessary. Process for another minute to make the dough elastic. Turn out onto the work surface and knead until smooth. Divide the dough in half, wrap in plastic wrap and rest for 20 minutes.

To make the almond filling, mix all the filling ingredients to form a stiff paste. Take 3 level teaspoons of filling and shape the filling into a ball. Continue in this manner, shaping the almond paste to make 30 balls of the same size. Oil your hands and roll each ball between your palms to form a torpedo shape 7.5 cm (3 in) long, tapering at each end. Place on baking paper and set aside. Preheat the oven to 180°C (350°F/Gas 4).

Roll out one ball of dough on a lightly floured work surface to a rectangle about 30 x 40 cm (12 x 16 in), with the longer side nearest you. Lay three almond shapes across the pastry, 5 cm (2 in) in from the bottom edge of the pastry (directly in front of you). They should be about 5 cm (2 in) apart and set in 3 cm (1¼ in) from each end. Lightly brush the pastry along the edge and between the almond filling with cold water. Turn the bottom edge of the pastry over the filling and press firmly around the filling to seal. Cut around the filling in a semi-circle with a fluted pastry wheel, leaving a 2 cm (¾ in) border. Place on a baking tray and bend upwards on the filling side to form a crescent. Straighten the edge of the pastry on the bench with a knife and repeat this process again until all the filling is used (reroll the pastry trimmings).

Bake for 15 minutes, or until lightly coloured. Transfer to a wire rack and dust with sifted icing sugar while hot. Store in an airtight container.

300 g (10½ oz/3 cups) ground almonds
150 g (5½ oz/1¼ cups) icing
  (confectioners') sugar
1½ teaspoons baking powder
½ teaspoon ground cinnamon
1 egg
2 teaspoons grated lemon zest
1 tablespoon rosewater
3 tablespoons icing (confectioners')
  sugar, extra

Makes 30–35

Put the ground almonds in a mixing bowl and sift in the icing sugar, baking powder and cinnamon. Stir well to mix the dry ingredients thoroughly. Beat the egg with the lemon zest and rosewater and add to the dry ingredients. Mix to a firm paste and knead lightly.

Line two baking trays with baking paper. Sift the extra icing sugar into a shallow dish. Preheat the oven to 180°C (350°F/Gas 4).

Break off pieces of dough the size of a walnut and roll into balls, oiling your hands lightly to prevent the dough sticking. Press the balls into the extra sifted icing sugar and flatten slightly. Lift carefully so that the topping is not disturbed, and place on the baking trays, sugar side up, spacing them 5 cm (2 in) apart to allow for spreading. Bake for 20 minutes. Leave the macaroons on the trays for 10 minutes before removing to a wire rack to cool. Store in an airtight container.

almond
macaroons

semolina biscuits

250 g (9 oz) unsalted butter
125 g (4½ oz/1 cup) plain (all-purpose)
   flour
125 g (4½ oz/1 cup) icing (confectioners')
   sugar
250 g (9 oz/2 cups) very fine semolina
2 eggs, beaten
1 teaspoon natural vanilla extract
1 egg white, lightly beaten
30 g (1 oz/¼ cup) split, blanched almonds
icing (confectioners') sugar, extra
   (optional)

Makes about 50

Melt the butter in a heavy-based saucepan over low heat. Skim off the froth, then pour into a mixing bowl, leaving the white milk solids in the pan. Set aside until cool.

Sift the flour and icing sugar into a bowl, add the semolina, a pinch of salt and mix thoroughly. When the butter is cool but still liquid, stir in the eggs and vanilla, then add the dry ingredients, mixing to a firm dough. Knead well, then cover the bowl with plastic wrap and leave for 1 hour. Line two baking trays with baking paper. Preheat the oven to 180°C (350°F/Gas 4).

Knead the dough again until smooth and pliant. Take 3 level teaspoons of dough and shape into a smooth ball, then shape the remaining dough into balls of the same size. Place on prepared trays 2.5 cm (1 in) apart, as these do not spread. Brush the tops lightly with egg white and press an almond on top of each biscuit, which will also help to flatten the biscuits a little. Bake for 20 minutes, or until lightly golden in colour. Cool on trays. When cold, sift the extra icing sugar on top, if using, and store in an airtight container.

3 eggs
3 tablespoons orange juice
3 tablespoons vegetable oil
1 tablespoon grated orange zest
60 g (2¼ oz/¼ cup) caster (superfine)
  sugar
300 g (10½ oz/2⅓ cups) plain
  (all-purpose) flour
1 teaspoon baking powder
about 4 tablespoons plain (all-purpose)
  flour, extra
vegetable oil, for deep-frying

SYRUP
2 tablespoons lemon juice
275 g (9¾ oz/1¼ oz) sugar
115 g (4 oz/⅓ cup) honey
1 tablespoon grated orange zest

Serves 4–6

Whisk the eggs, orange juice and oil together in a large bowl. Add the orange zest and sugar and whisk until frothy. Sift in the flour and baking powder and mix with a wooden spoon until smooth, but still a bit sticky. Cover and set aside for 1 hour.

To make the syrup, put 310 ml (10¾ fl oz/1¼ cups) cold water, the lemon juice and sugar in a saucepan and heat, stirring until the sugar dissolves. Bring to the boil, reduce the heat and simmer for 5 minutes. Add the honey and orange zest and simmer for another 5 minutes. Keep warm.

Sprinkle a little of the extra flour onto the dough and transfer it to a lightly floured surface. Work in just enough extra flour to give a dough that doesn't stick to your hands. Roll out to a thickness of 5 mm (¼ in). It will be very elastic, so keep rolling and resting it until it stops shrinking. Using a 5 cm (2 in) biscuit cutter, cut out round cakes.

Heat the oil in a large deep-sided frying pan to 170°C (325°F), or until a cube of bread dropped into the oil browns in 20 seconds. Fry the cakes three or four at a time until puffed and golden—about 1 minute on each side. Remove with tongs and drain on paper towels.

Using tongs, dip each cake into the warm honey syrup, long enough for it to soak in. Transfer to a platter. Serve warm or cold.

fried honey cakes

dates... According to a Moroccan saying, date palms must have their heads in fire and their feet in water — the hot Moroccan sun to bring the fruit to succulent sweetness, and ground water for their roots.

The date has sustained the desert nomads for countless centuries. It still sustains those who have not given up their traditional existence, and is just as important to villagers and city dwellers. For food on the move, the date is difficult to beat — an instant boost of energy with its high sugar content, and a little protein, vitamins and minerals thrown in. Taking a year to mature, fresh dates make their appearance in the *souks* in December, arranged painstakingly in mini pyramids. Hues vary from light golden brown, through red-brown to a rich

chocolate. There are dates ready for eating immediately, dates for cooking and dates to have on hand for snacking.

As well as its fruit, the date palm provides fronds, which are dried and used for baskets and table mats; the fibre from its bark is made into ropes; the stones of the fruit are used for fuel; and the trunk is used for timber. Date palms can produce fruit for 60 years; however, they can exceed 30 metres (100 feet) in height and are cut down when harvesting becomes too difficult. In the Erfoud oasis alone, one million date palms flourish, encompassing 30 varieties. The average annual yield is about 45 kg (100 lb) of fruit per tree.

Muslims regard the date palm as the tree of life — it is easy to see why.

briouats with dates

125 g (4½ oz) smen (page 247), melted
165 g (5¾ oz/1 cup) blanched almonds
80 g (2¾ oz/½ cup) pitted, chopped dates
80 g (2¾ oz/½ cup) chopped dessert figs
    (soft, dried figs)

1 tablespoon orange flower water
12–14 sheets filo pastry
icing (confectioners') sugar, to serve

Makes 18

In a small frying pan, warm 1 tablespoon of the smen, add the almonds and cook over medium heat, stirring often, until golden. Tip immediately into the food processor bowl, along with the smen in the pan. When the almonds are cool, process until finely chopped, then add the dates, figs and orange flower water and process to a thick paste, scraping down the side of the bowl as necessary. Turn out onto the work surface, rub your hands with a little of the smen and gather the paste into a ball. Roll into a sausage 23 cm (9 in) long and cut into 18 equal pieces. Roll each piece into a short cigar shape 10 cm (4 in) long. Place on a sheet of baking paper and set aside.

Count out 12 sheets of filo pastry (if the pastry is shorter than 39 cm (15½ in) in length, you will need extra sheets). Stack the filo on a cutting surface and, with a ruler and sharp knife, measure and cut across the width through the stack to give strips 12–13 cm (4½–5 in) wide and 28–30 cm (11¼–12 in) long. Stack the cut filo in the folds of a dry tea towel (dish towel) or cover with plastic wrap.

Place a strip of pastry with the narrow end nearest you and brush with the warm, melted smen. Top with another strip and brush with melted smen. Put the shaped filling 1 cm (½ in) in from the base and about 1.5 cm (⅝ in) in from the sides of the strip. Fold the end of the filo over the filling, fold in the sides and brush the side folds with smen. Roll to the end and place, seam side down, on a greased baking tray. Repeat with the remaining ingredients. Preheat the oven to 180°C (350°F/Gas 4) after the briouats are completed to keep the kitchen cool while shaping.

Brush the tops of the briouats lightly with smen and bake in the preheated oven for 20 minutes until lightly golden. Sift icing sugar over them while still hot. When cool, store in a sealed container. The rolls keep for 2 days stored at room temperature.

1 ripe avocado, about 225 g (8 oz)
1½ tablespoons caster (superfine) sugar
375 ml (13 fl oz/1½ cups) chilled milk
½ teaspoon orange flower water

Serves 2

Halve the avocado and put it in a blender, then add the sugar and chilled milk. Blend until smooth and frothy. Taste and add more sugar if necessary. Add the orange flower water, blend briefly and pour into two tall glasses. Serve immediately.

avocado
sharbat

basics

SAFFRON RICE

500 g (1 lb 2 oz/2½ cups) long-grain rice
½ teaspoon ground saffron threads
2 tablespoons olive oil
20 g (¾ oz) butter
60 g (2¼ oz/⅔ cup) flaked almonds, toasted,
    to garnish (optional)

Serves 6

Wash the rice in a sieve until the water runs clear, then drain well. Bring 900 ml (31 fl oz) water to the boil and add the saffron. Allow the saffron to infuse for 20 minutes.

Heat the olive oil in a heavy-based saucepan and add the rice, stirring well so that all the rice is coated evenly in the oil. Add the saffron water and ¼ teaspoon salt and stir well. Bring to the boil and boil for 1 minute.

Cover with a tight-fitting lid, then reduce the heat to as low as possible and cook for 10–12 minutes, or until all the water has been absorbed. Steam tunnels will form holes on the surface of the rice. Turn off the heat, then leave the pan covered for at least 10 minutes. Add the butter and fluff lightly with a fork. Scatter with the almonds, if using them, and serve.

SMEN

250 g (9 oz) salted or unsalted butter

Makes 175 g (6 oz)

Cut the butter into pieces and place in a heavy-based saucepan over low heat.
If using gas, place over the smallest burner with a heat diffuser, as butter has a
tendency to spit if the heat is not low enough.

Simmer very gently for 25 minutes. Pour through a sieve lined with muslin (cheesecloth),
set over a bowl. The clear oil is the smen and has a slightly nutty taste. Store in a
sealed jar in the refrigerator, although it can safely be stored at room temperature,
as is done in Morocco. This keeps for many months.

For sweet pastries using filo, smen (clarified butter) is recommended, even with its
slightly nutty flavour, because if melted unclarified butter is used any milk solids
brushed onto the filo become dark when cooked, spoiling the appearance of the
baked pastry.

HERBED SMEN

**2 tablespoons dried za'atar or
  dried Greek thyme**
2 teaspoons coarse salt
250 g (9 oz) salted or unsalted butter

Makes 175 g (6 oz)

Put the za'atar or thyme and salt in sieve lined with muslin (cheesecloth). Following
the directions above, heat the butter and pour it through the herb mixture. Store in
a sealed jar in the refrigerator. Herbed smen is aged for months, even years, in
Morocco and has a strong, cheesy flavour. This is a milder version.

COUSCOUS (STEAMING METHOD)

450 g (1 lb/2½ cups) couscous
90 g (3¼ oz) butter, diced

Serves 6–8

Couscous purchased in bulk, and packets of instant couscous should be prepared in the same way for best results. Both require steaming for the grains to swell properly and become light and fluffy.

Put the couscous in a large, shallow bowl, cover with cold water, stir with your fingers and pour the water off immediately through a strainer to catch any grains. Return the grains to the bowl and set aside for 15 minutes to allow the couscous to swell. Rake the couscous with your fingers to separate the grains.

Use the steamer section of a couscoussier or a steamer that fits snugly over a large saucepan. If the steamer does not fit snugly, put a long, folded strip of foil around the rim of the pan, place the steamer in position and press firmly. A metal colander may also be used with this method of sealing in the steam.

Line the steamer with a double layer of muslin (cheesecloth), add the swollen couscous grains and place over the pan of food being cooked (such as a stew), or over a saucepan of boiling water. The base of the steamer must not touch the top of the food or water. Cook, uncovered, until the steam rises through the grains and steam for 20 minutes. Fork through the couscous occasionally to steam it evenly.

Tip the couscous into a large bowl, add the butter and ½ teaspoon salt and sprinkle with 125 ml (4 fl oz/½ cup) cold water. Toss through the couscous and, when cool enough, lightly rub handfuls of couscous to break up the lumps. At this stage, the couscous may be covered with a damp cloth and left for several hours if necessary. About 20 minutes before the stew is cooked, return the couscous to the muslin-lined steamer and replace over the stew or boiling water. Do not cover. Fluff up occasionally with a fork.

This is the traditional way to prepare couscous and gives the best results. If you are short of time, you can use the microwave method (page 249) or, alternatively, prepare the couscous following the instructions on the packet.

COUSCOUS (MICROWAVE METHOD)

450 g (1 lb/2½ cups) couscous
90 g (3¼ oz) butter, diced

Serves 6–8

Put the couscous in a large 3 litre (105 fl oz/12 cup) glass or ceramic casserole dish, cover with cold water, drain, then set aside for 15 minutes. Rake your fingers through the couscous to separate the grains.

Have 625 ml (21½ fl oz/2½ cups) water measured out. Pour about a third of the water over the couscous, cover and microwave on full power for 3 minutes, then fluff with a fork and microwave for 2 minutes. Fluff thoroughly with the fork to break up the lumps, sprinkle with another third of the water and microwave for 3 minutes. Add the butter and ½ teaspoon salt, fork the couscous thoroughly and add the remaining water. Stir through and microwave for a further 3 minutes. Fork once again and set aside, covered, until required. Couscous can be reheated in the microwave if necessary before serving.

To microwave smaller quantities of couscous, use equal amounts by volume of couscous and water, use a smaller container and reduce cooking times. Timing is not crucial, but gradually adding the water and forking the couscous to break up the lumps is important. The result should be light, fluffy grains, with the couscous more than three times its original volume.

HARISSA

125 g (4½ oz) dried red chillies,
 stems removed
1 tablespoon dried mint
1 tablespoon ground coriander
1 tablespoon ground cumin

1 teaspoon ground caraway seeds
10 garlic cloves, chopped
125 ml (4 fl oz/½ cup) olive oil

Fills a 600 ml (21 fl oz) jar

To prepare a storage jar, preheat the oven to 120°C (235°F/Gas ½). Wash the jar and lid in hot soapy water and rinse with hot water. Put the jar in the oven for 20 minutes, or until fully dry. Do not dry with a tea towel (dish towel).

Roughly chop the chillies, then cover with boiling water and soak for 1 hour. Drain, put them in a food processor and add the mint, spices, garlic, 1 tablespoon of the olive oil and ½ teaspoon salt. Process for 20 seconds, scrape down the side of the bowl, then process for another 30 seconds. With the motor running, gradually add the remaining oil, scraping down the side of the bowl when necessary.

Spoon the paste into the clean jar, cover with a thin layer of olive oil and seal. Label and date. Harissa will keep in the refrigerator for up to 6 months.

RAS EL HANOUT

½ teaspoon ground cloves
½ teaspoon ground cayenne pepper
2 teaspoons ground allspice
2 teaspoons ground cumin
2 teaspoons ground ginger
2 teaspoons ground turmeric

2 teaspoons ground black pepper
2 teaspoons ground cardamom
3 teaspoons ground cinnamon
3 teaspoons ground coriander
2 nutmegs, freshly grated
 (or 6 teaspoons ground nutmeg)

To make your own spice mixture, combine all the ground spices and store in a tightly sealed jar.

PRESERVED LEMONS

8–12 small thin-skinned new-season lemons
310 g (11 oz/1 cup) rock salt
500 ml (17 fl oz/2 cups) lemon juice (you will
    need 8–10 lemons)
½ teaspoon black peppercorns
1 bay leaf
olive oil

Fills 1 x 2 litre (70 fl oz/8 cup) jar or
    2 x 1 litre (35 fl oz/4 cup) jars

To prepare a storage jar, preheat the oven to 120°C (235°F/Gas ½). Wash the jar and lid in hot soapy water and rinse with hot water. Put the jar in the oven for 20 minutes, or until fully dry. Do not dry with a tea towel (dish towel). Use a jar that has a clip or a tight-fitting lid.

Scrub the lemons under warm running water with a soft bristle brush to remove the wax coating. Cut into quarters, leaving the base attached at the stem end. Gently open each lemon, remove any visible seeds and pack 1 tablespoon of the rock salt against the cut edges of each lemon. Push the lemons back into shape and pack tightly into the prepared jar. Depending on the size of the lemons, you may not need all 12. They should be firmly packed and fill the jar.

Add 250 ml (9 fl oz/1 cup) of the lemon juice, peppercorns, bay leaf and remaining salt to the jar. Fill the jar to the top with the remaining lemon juice. Seal and shake to combine all the ingredients. Leave in a cool, dark place for 6 weeks, inverting the jar each week. The liquid will be cloudy initially, but will clear by the fourth week.

To test if the lemons are preserved, cut through the centre of one of the lemon quarters. If the pith is still white, the lemons aren't ready. In this case, re-seal and leave for another week before testing again. The lemons should be soft-skinned and the pith should be the same colour as the skin.

Once the lemons are preserved, cover the brine with a layer of olive oil. Replace the oil each time you remove some of the lemon pieces. Refrigerate after opening. Both the rind and the underlying pith 'sweeten' during the pickling process. Discard the pulp and membranes, then rinse and thinly slice or chop the rind before adding to the dish. Preserved lemons can be stored for up to 6 months in a cool, dark place.

glossary

almonds Whole, slivered and ground almonds are often used in sweet and savoury dishes. If ground almonds are not available, use whole or slivered almonds and grind in a food processor. Use very fresh, dry almonds for this, and process them as briefly as possible to prevent them from becoming oily. Pack well when using cup measures, as freshly ground almonds are lighter in texture than the ready-made version.

broad (fava) beans Only very young fresh, shelled beans are used in tagines. Dried broad beans are often used to make a bean dip. If using dried broad beans, they need to be first soaked and the leathery skins removed before use. Dried, skinned broad beans are sold in Middle Eastern food markets and will save time in preparation.

chickpeas Skinned chickpeas are preferred as they absorb flavours better. Soak chickpeas overnight; the next day, lift up handfuls of chickpeas and rub them between your hands to loosen the skins, then skim the skins off as they float. Cover the chickpeas with fresh water and boil for at least an hour, until tender, or add to a stew or soup at the start of cooking. Canned chickpeas may also be used, with skins removed in the same way. If preferred, leave skins on

for all recipes. 220 g (7¾ oz/1 cup) dried chickpeas yields 2½ cups cooked chickpeas, which is equivalent to 2 x 420 g (15 oz) tins.

cinnamon Finely shaved bark from the cinnamon tree, *Cinnamomum zeylanicum*, which is interleaved and rolled to form sticks or quills. Both sticks and ground cinnamon are widely used. Ground cinnamon often includes cassia, which is actually from another species of cinnamon tree. Cassia is more reddish-brown than cinnamon and can be used in place of cinnamon stick; in fact, it is often sold as such. Cinnamon is used in savoury and sweet dishes and pastries.

coriander (cilantro) Essential in Moroccan cooking, fresh coriander has feathery green leaves with a somewhat pungent flavour. Coriander seeds are ground and used as a spice.

couscous Made with coarse semolina grains and durum wheat flour. The semolina grains are sprinkled with lightly salted water and rolled in flour to form tiny pellets. This is still done by hand by some cooks, but machines now make it. Couscous purchased in bulk, and packets of instant couscous should be prepared in the same way for best results. Both

require steaming for the grains to swell properly and become light and fluffy.

couscoussier A tall cooking pot, slightly bulbous, with a steamer section fitted on top for cooking couscous. The traditional couscoussier of tin-lined copper does not have a lid, but the aluminium ones do. The original couscoussier of the Berbers was earthenware.

gum arabic Little tears of dried sap from *Acacia arabica* and other trees of the family *Mimosoideae*. It is crushed and used in some pastries, especially in Marrakesh, and fumes from burning gum arabic are used to flavour water.

harissa A Tunisian condiment, popular in Morocco. It is made with soaked, dried chillies and spices, but Moroccans also make a mild harissa by including roasted sweet red capsicum (pepper). Harissa is available from gourmet food stores and Middle Eastern markets, or make your own (page 250). Use with caution as it is extremely hot.

honey Good Moroccan honeys are thick and aromatic with the flavour of herbs. If you can't find Moroccan honey, use Mount Hymettus or other Greek thyme honey. Orange blossom honey is light and fragrant and is readily available.

merguez A lamb sausage of Tunisian origin, popular in Morocco. It is spiced with harissa, paprika, allspice, fennel, black pepper, cumin and coriander seeds and flavoured with garlic. It is usually very hot, but the degree of heat depends on the manufacturer.

olive oil Olive oil was, and is, used for salads, but there is an increasing trend in Morocco to replace smen in cooking with olive or other oil in the interests of better health. While no distinction has been made in recipes regarding type of oil, extra virgin olive oil is recommended for salads, and the standard olive oil for cooking. Other vegetable oils are usually used for frying.

orange flower water Also called orange blossom water, this is made from a distillation of the flowers of the bitter orange. It originated in the Middle East and was introduced to North Africa by the Arabs. Used to flavour beverages, and sweet and savoury food.

paprika The paprika commonly used is Spanish mild paprika. It is used as much for the colour it imparts as its flavour.

parsley Flat-leaf (Italian) parsley is used. Alternatively, use curly parsley and include some stalks when chopping to increase its flavour in cooking.

preserved lemons Used in tagines and many Moroccan dishes to give a distinctive flavour. Make your own (page 251) or buy those that are preserved only in salt from gourmet food stores or good delicatessens.

quince A popular winter fruit used in tagines. While quince paste is not made in Morocco, it works very well in recipes when quinces are not in season.

ras el hanout A blend of many spices, which vary according to the maker. Some blends are kept a closely guarded secret. You can make your own version (page 250) or buy a ready-made ground spice mix from gourmet food stores or good delicatessens.

rosewater A distillation of fragrant rose petals, originating in Persia and introduced to North Africa by the Arabs. Used to flavour beverages and sweet and savoury foods.

saffron The dried stigmas of *Crocus sativus*, and regarded as the world's most expensive spice. Each flower consists of only a few stigmas, which are hand-picked, then dried. Introduced by the Arabs, it is grown, harvested and processed in Morocco. Threads and ground saffron are used as much for the beautiful yellow colour as for the flavour. Where a recipe calls for a pinch of ground saffron, use as much as sits on the very tip of a knife, as fingertips would take more than required. Take care when buying saffron—if it's cheap, it's probably not real saffron.

semolina The milled inner endosperm of hard or durum wheat, pale beige or yellow in colour and granular in appearance. It can be very fine (almost like a flour), fine or coarse, the latter used in the manufacture of couscous. Fine and coarse semolina are sold as breakfast cereals. Very fine semolina is available at markets selling Middle Eastern and Greek foods. Do not confuse semolina with semolina flour, which is used in pasta making, and is durum wheat flour.

smen A clarified (drawn) butter with milk solids that have been allowed to brown slightly, giving it a slightly nutty flavour (page 247). An aged smen is made by the Berbers by storing the smen in a sealed earthenware jar, which is then stored in the cellar or buried for a year or longer until it ages; it has a flavour resembling strong blue cheese. Ghee can be used as a substitute.

yeast Active dried yeast is available in bulk or in sealed 8 g (¼ oz) sachets that measure 2 teaspoons. Always store yeast in a sealed container in the refrigerator and use within its use-by date. If yeast has been correctly stored but is past its use-by date, dissolve a teaspoon of the yeast in 125 ml (4 fl oz/ ½ cup) warm water with 1 teaspoon sugar and leave in a warm place for 15 minutes. If it is frothy in this time, the yeast can be used, otherwise discard it.

za'atar Arabic word for thyme. The Mediterranean climate gives certain wild herbs a pungency and flavour difficult to duplicate with cultivated herbs. If you cannot find dried za'atar from Morocco in food markets, use the dried thyme available at Greek markets or use fresh lemon thyme; recipes indicate which substitutes are suitable. Do not confuse this with the Lebanese herb and spice mix of za'atar, used to sprinkle on bread.

index

Published in 2006 by Murdoch Books Pty Limited
www.murdochbooks.com.au

Murdoch Books Australia
Pier 8/9, 23 Hickson Road, Millers Point NSW 2000
Phone: +61 (0)2 8220 2000   Fax: +61 (0)2 8220 2558

Murdoch Books UK Limited
Erico House, 6th Floor, 93–99 Upper Richmond Road
Putney, London SW15 2TG
Phone: +44 (0)20 8785 5995   Fax: +44 (0)20 8785 5985

Chief Executive: Juliet Rogers
Publisher: Kay Scarlett

Design Concept: Vivien Valk
Designer: Susanne Geppert
Project Manager: Margaret Malone
Editor: Kim Rowney
Food Editor: Jane Lawson
Photographers: Ashley Mackevicius (recipes), Martin Brigdale (location)
Stylist: Wendy Berecry
Food preparation: Ross Dobson
Recipes and text: Tess Mallos
Additional recipes: Murdoch Books Test Kitchen
Production: Adele Troeger

National Library of Australia Cataloguing-in-Publication Data
Mallos, Tess. A little taste of Morocco. Includes index.
ISBN 978 1 74045 754 5
1. Cookery, Moroccan. I. Title. 641.5964

Printed by Midas Printing (Asia) Ltd. PRINTED IN CHINA. Reprinted 2007 (three times), 2008.

©Text, design and photography Murdoch Books Pty Limited 2006. All rights reserved. No part of this publication may be reproduced, stored in a retrieval system or transmitted in any form or by any means, electronic, mechanical, photocopying, recording or otherwise without the prior written permission of the publisher.

Material in this book has previously appeared in *Cooking Moroccan*.

IMPORTANT: Those who might be at risk from the effects of salmonella poisoning (the elderly, pregnant women, young children and those suffering from immune deficiency diseases) should consult their doctor with any concerns about eating raw eggs.

CONVERSION GUIDE: You may find cooking times vary depending on the oven you are using. For fan-forced ovens, as a general rule, set the oven temperature to 20°C (35°F) lower than indicated in the recipe. We have used 20 ml (4 teaspoon) tablespoon measures. If you are using a 15 ml (3 teaspoon) tablespoon, for most recipes the difference will not be noticeable. However, for recipes using baking powder, gelatine, bicarbonate of soda (baking soda), small amounts of flour and cornflour (cornstarch), add an extra teaspoon for each tablespoon specified.